Fish House Opera

Susan West *and*
Barbara J. Garrity-Blake

Best fismes —
Love,
Susan West
June 2012

MYSTIC SEAPORT.
THE MUSEUM OF AMERICA AND THE SEA ™

Mystic Seaport
75 Greenmanville Ave., P.O. Box 6000
Mystic, CT 06355-0990

Cataloging-in-Publication Data

West, Susan B.
    Fish house opera / Susan West and Barbara J. Garrity-Blake.—
Mystic, Conn. : Mystic Seaport, 2003.
        p. : ill., maps, ports. ; cm.
        "Sources": p.

    1. Fishers—North Carolina. 2. Fishery processing industries—North
Carolina—Employees. 3. Fishery management—United States—Case
studies. 4. North Carolina—Social conditions. I. Garrity-Blake, Barbara J.,
1960- II. Title.

HD8039.F66U5 2003

ISBN 0-913372-99-4

Designed by Linda Cusano

This book is dedicated to
Rob West and Bryan Blake

Table of Contents

Prologue

The door to the post office swung open and a large man shouted, "Susan, give me a book of stamps." Fuel receipts, a telephone bill, and a few nuts and bolts littered the lobby counter as Kendall Gray emptied the contents of his pants pockets searching for cash.

"When's the price going up?" asked Kendall, checking his T-shirt pocket. I opened my mouth but before I could say a word, Kendall fired another question at me. "All the mail hauled over?" This expression, left-over from the time when the mail came by boat and was literally hauled over from boat to shore, identified Kendall as a native son of Kinnakeet, an Outer Banks village that lost its lyric Indian name on the whim of some bureaucrat who christened the place Avon.

Before I could tell him that yes, all the mail has been sorted into the post office boxes, Kendall muttered, "Now, damn, what did I do with that money? Have you heard anything about flounder fishing? When are they going to close it down? Man, I can't believe what they're doing to these boys. I'm still crabbing. It was pretty work for a while but now the price has gone to hell. How's Rob doing? Is he still Spanish fishing? Heard those fellas got into the meat yesterday. Oh, here's that money. Thanks."

People on Hatteras Island talk fish to me. A netter complains that the state has reneged on its promise of an increased quota once the striped bass fishery was restored. The wife of a fisherman confides, " I just hope our sons can get through college before the government shuts down fishing for good." An optimistic tackle-shop owner tells me, "You know, I really think we can work out this squabble between the commercials and the recreationals, don't you?"

What makes this all so strange is that I'm not a fisherman. I've never worked on a commercial boat and I've fished for fun only a handful of times. But my friends and neighbors talk fish with me because I'm married to a commercial fisherman who encouraged my foray into the world of fisheries management and fish politics nearly a decade ago. At that time a small group of fishermen's wives formed a grass-roots organization serving the fishing families of Hatteras and Ocracoke Islands. Looking back, I don't know whether to laugh or cry over how naïve our group was in the beginning, before our idealism ran headlong into political blockades. My level of activism has waxed and waned through the years, but here I am a decade later, still lifting a finger to check which way the political winds are blowing.

I hang my hat with fishermen who say they didn't learn about fish from behind a computer or at a university. Academic curiosity didn't drive me to say yes when Barbara asked whether we might write this book together. This book is very personal for me. It's the story of my husband, my friends, and my neighbors.

Susan West
Buxton, North Carolina
September 2002

I sat next to a gruff veteran of Carolina politics at a seafood banquet held at the state's marine fisheries facility in Morehead City. Marine fisheries staff hosted the feast in hopes that the political bigwigs from Raleigh would ingest a kindly attitude and appropriate more funds to their agency. The legislators had already been taken on a boat tour and were happy to relax in the marine patrol helicopter hanger as "fish cops" served up bushels and barrels of shrimp, scallops, and deep-fried hushpuppies.

The politician congratulated me on my recent appointment to the state's fisheries commission and asked me about research that I had done for a Ph.D. in anthropology. "You studied fish factories right here instead of some tribe in the South Seas?"

Okay, I thought. Here's a chance to show my stuff and put in a good word for fishermen. "That's right," I said to the legislator. "In fact, I wrote a book about the fishmeal and oil industry."

"And it's all lies!" said a voice behind me. Jule Wheatly, owner and manager of the last remaining fish factory in North Carolina, had showed up at the banquet. He shook hands all around and took a seat at the end of the table. "Yup. She left out all the good parts." He tilted his chair back and fought a smile, eyes laughing. I knew what was coming next. "Listen! She shows up at the factory, barefoot with a backpack, and I couldn't get rid of her for a solid year. Just like a stray cat! Had to feed her Cokes and Nabs so she wouldn't starve." All right, I told myself. Might as well give it up. Nobody in Carteret County passes a chance to knock you off your high horse. "And aggravating? My God in this world! She asked more questions. Drove us all plumb crazy."

"I loved doing fieldwork at the fish factory," I said, attempting to salvage just a shred of dignity. "It was one of the best experiences of my life."

Wheatly rocked his chair forward and hooted. "My Lord honey, if crawling around a fish factory was one of the best times of your life, you have had one sorry life!" He slapped the table with delight. "If I were you I'd just throw myself off the Morehead bridge and end it all!"

I surrendered with laugher as the conversation mercifully drifted. I found myself still laughing on my drive home to Gloucester. Beyond all the fishery research, facts, numbers, and figures lay a lot of heart and humor in the people who make up the industry. From the top of the Morehead bridge I could just make out the menhaden factory smoke stacks in Beaufort, as well as a steel trawler heading out to the Atlantic Ocean. I could also see a new condominium going up on Radio Island, and rafts of sportfishing boats and sailboats tied up at marinas. It struck me how the very culture and history that shaped coastal towns can be invisible to newcomers, as if a fading backdrop to life at the beach.

Yet there is no lack of information about fisheries issues—my desk, kitchen table, and couches are frequently covered with sliding heaps of articles, studies, management plans, tapes, and transcripts. In the midst of writing this book, Susan and I became overwhelmed trying not to leave anything out, and realized that too much information can obscure the essence of what's going on. Our challenge was not to piece together all the details, nor to orchestrate the many voices that have something to say about coastal issues, but to distill the information and quiet the noise so as to portray precisely who and what gets lost in the shuffle.

Fragile little worlds rooted in salt marsh and mud still thrive, against terrific odds, from Maine to the Gulf of Mexico to Oregon, in heart-breaking testimony to American perseverance. The story is heartbreaking, as every fisherman in the U.S. knows, because it is being revised and rewritten by those powerful enough to change whole landscapes and influence the views of large numbers of people. But fishermen, mediators between the ever boxed-in and regulated life of society and the flux and fluidity of life on the water, manage to keep bringing us the only wild food product on the U.S. market. Fishing families live by the values considered truly American—independence, risk-taking, and freedom—and get punished for having the audacity to do so. May this scrappy group of survivors sail into the future and garner a little more respect and fairness in the world.

Barbara Garrity-Blake
Gloucester, North Carolina
September 2002

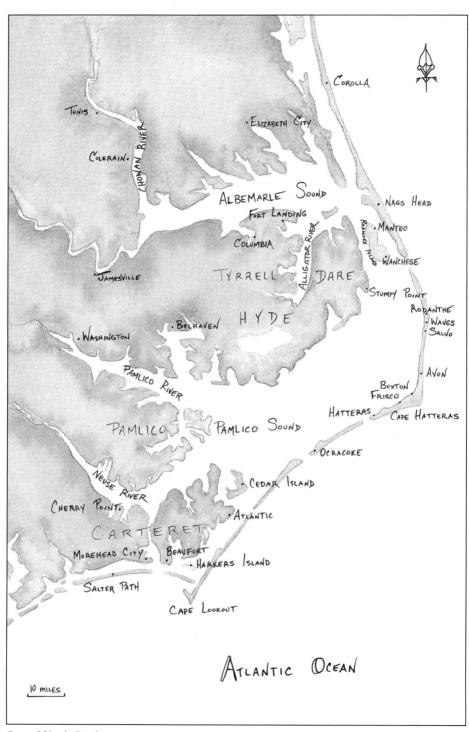

Coastal North Carolina.
Map © Sally Anger

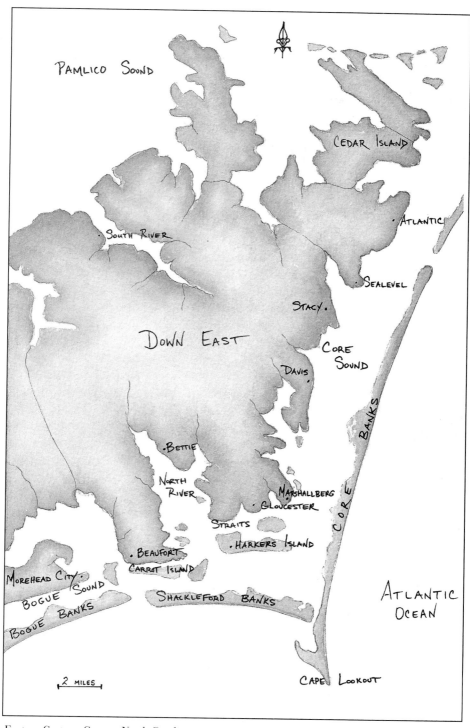

Eastern Carteret County, North Carolina.
Map © Sally Anger

"Prisoners of Commercial Fishing Regulations."
Photo by B. Garrity-Blake

Boom Truck
Heaven

Sirens shattered the easy beat of waves lapping the shore. Locals and off-the-beaten-path curiosity seekers slid from the hoods of cars, called their children off the road, and checked their cameras. Everyone looked down the twisted lane, between the gnarled oaks and longleaf pines. A boy popping wheelies held the bike still; his breath hanging in short puffs in the February air. A man wearing a flannel coat lifted a toddler to his left shoulder. Children stood on tiptoe or darted daringly into the empty road and back.

A herky-jerky monster rounded the bend and the crowd caught their first glimpse of the boom truck parade, a metallic blaze of vehicles festooned with banners, flags, and steamy smoke. The crowd sang out in hoots and howls as the motley procession approached, escorted by a Cedar Island Volunteer Fire Department engine. Unique spray-painted designs and crepe-paper frills adorned each truck, but all the decorations in the world couldn't have masked the scars from punishing labor in the no-nonsense world of fishing.

"For those of you who don't know what a boom truck is," wrote Cedar Island reporter Ed Butler, "and that's most of mankind, it's a rusty old pickup truck in whose bed is installed a battery-powered winch used for heavy lifting." The boom is usually welded onto an otherwise retired truck, but "Benny Styron once crammed a boom into the trunk of his sorry Oldsmobile and it worked just fine."

Boom trucks are as natural to Carteret County fishing villages as skiffs in the yard, nets webbed between trees, and stacks of crab pots piled beside sheds. The mechanical workhorses tug heavy diesel engines out of vessels, toss pound nets onto boats, and yank tree stumps out of the ground. These street trawlers are the fishermen's jury-rigged beasts of burden, born out of necessity and kept alive by whatever it takes—daily quarts of oil, bailing wire, duct tape. Some boom trucks haven't seen an inspection sticker in years, and chug from house to dock in Cedar Island like junkyard refugees with a second lease on life. Despite their great utility, fishermen never considered the lowly and taken-for-granted boom truck worthy of celebration. That changed in 1996.

When he came to Cedar Island's United Methodist Church, Reverend Bob Carpenter found himself charmed by the remote fishing village he now ministered. Six bridges from the town of Beaufort, via a meandering two-lane road through the villages of Bettie, Otway, Smyrna, Davis, and Stacy, past wide expanses of marsh and knots of yaupon and myrtle bushes, lies Cedar Island–the farthest flung and eastern most point of "Down East" Carteret County.

Down East is named from pre-bridge days, when villagers sailed wooden sharpies and skiffs to Beaufort for supplies, then set their snow-white sails for home eastward toward Harkers Island and beyond. "I'd ride all the way on the mailboat from Beaufort to Cedar Island where my grandmother lived," recalled historian Thelma Simpson. First inhabited by Coree Indians, then English settlers, water-bound villages like Harkers Island, Marshallberg, Atlantic, and Cedar Island retain their uniqueness, especially in the villagers' clipped Elizabethan brogue. "One day when I was a little girl visiting, it was the lowest tide," Simpson reflected. "My grandmother asked, 'Why don't you go crabbing?' She fixed me an old dishpan, tied a string on it, and said 'Just drag this along behind you, and every little hole you see, rake that seaweed away and you'll find a crab.' Directly I had that dishpan full of crabs and Grandmother couldn't believe it. She supplied everyone with crabs."

Cedar Islanders no longer survive solely on gardens, livestock, barters, and generosities. But a spirit of neighborliness and trust prevails. Few people lock their doors or bother removing car keys from ignitions. The tranquility of Cedar Island was briefly shattered in 1986 when retired postmaster Ralph Ray Palmer was shot seven times. Local songwriter Red Daniels, heartbroken by his friend's murder, immortalized Palmer in the ballad "Eureka, I've Found It." "The boy that murdered Ralphie wasn't from here," Red Daniels said, his prized American National guitar in his lap. "He was imported."

If not for the state ferry terminal at the end of Cedar Island, launching loads of people to Ocracoke and Hatteras Island, few tourists would run across the boom truck capital of the world. But Cedar Island's salty flavor impressed Reverend Carpenter. He had been transported to a place and time where no one had much money but everyone knew the names of each other's in-laws, children, and dogs. He noticed that the islanders communicated with few words, throwing a couple of fingers up to wave at a passerby, speaking well-worn shorthand at the general store, and reading volumes from each other's glances. But the community's idyllic surface did not blind him to a hint of unease that played around the eyes of villagers. "Everyday I look into the faces of these people, the fishermen," Carpenter reflected. "It is as if I can see the end of them."

It did not take the Reverend long to sense an undertow beneath the stillness of Cedar Island life. It pulled strongest in the winter months, when harsh nor'easters kept boats tied to docks and restless men home. "Supposed to clear up directly," husbands say to wives, trying not to think about unpaid Christmas bills and depleted bank accounts. Most fishermen, raised to make do with what they have, wait out the bad blows and choppy seas. Others, driven by the saltwater in their veins and unbearably thin wallets, do not. "If you listen to the weather you'll starve," fishermen say. "If you don't listen to it you'll drown."

The *Josephine* had seen better days. She was a rickety wooden trawler whose swelled hold had been filled with fish and shrimp a thousand times over. Some say the Pamlico County boat had no business plying the unfriendly February seas off Beaufort, while others say the captain had little choice. "People may wonder why the crew of the *Josephine* were out in such weather," said fisherman Doc Saunders of Atlantic. "The answer is the system. Short seasons on flounder fishing have caused a rush to work in the few winter days that are allowed." Saunders referred to a federal management system that apportioned each state a quota on the pounds of flounder that could be landed. The quota could be filled in a matter of days—if fishermen did not catch their share, they would be shut out until the next season. They no longer had the luxury of waiting for smooth seas and clear skies.

"Either work regardless of weather conditions," said Saunders, laying out the choices, "or don't work at all."

The captain and crew of the *Josephine* were towing for flounder when the sky threw a tantrum and the seas cranked up. The vessel, tossed about like a bathtub toy, simply came apart. No one survived, and one body was never found.

"She broke up about fifteen miles off Cape Lookout," said Carteret County storyteller Sonny Williamson. "A forty-foot section of the boat washed ashore a few weeks after Hurricane Bonnie. I had the honor of transporting the family out to Cape Lookout to see the remains of that vessel."

"Who's to blame for this?" asked Doc Saunders. Tough questions always followed a tragedy at sea. Could the captain have used better

The Honey Wagon.
Photo by B. Garrity-Blake

judgement? Could policymakers be a little flexible in their rulings, especially for winter fisheries? Could the Coast Guard have acted faster? "I guess all of us are to blame," he concluded.

Only days before the *Josephine* went down, the Boom Truck parade took place. Reverend Carpenter chose a Saturday in February as a diversion for restless watermen.

"We wanted to give the fishermen some way of breaking the February monotony," he said, explaining the odd parade. "Fishermen are workaholics and the wintertime is tough. We needed to do something to overcome their cabin fever." Time seems to crawl in February when the cold leaches the color out of the sea and turns the marsh brown–all the better to set off the garrish colors of a dressed-up boom truck.

Like a scene out of *The Road Warrior*, the boom trucks, tires screeching and engines groaning, chugged towards the crowd. One truck bumped into another and nobody seemed to care. A blur of rust, busted headlights, missing doors, and swinging hooks and chains rushed past the crowd. Wet paint, plastic alligators, "area closed to fishing" signs, and Confederate flags were the regalia of the day. Some entrants barely met the contest's only rule: trucks had to be self-propelled, not pushed, dragged, or rolled.

Imprisoned children waved from their cage on the back of "Jail Boom Truck," a white pickup bedecked with black spray-painted bars. "Prisoners of commercial fishing regulations" was written on the doors. The young jailbirds tossed smiles and hard candy to the crowd, their prison on wheels covered in black balloons and a sign that read, "keep us free."

The "Honey Wagon" was a ribald display featuring a septic pump ridden by a life-sized inflatable woman. The doll, popping out of a toilet seat, looked shocked to be wearing a bikini in February.

"Boom Truck Heaven" won Best in Show. The truck was an unearthly mix of angel wings, greasy cables, halos, and heavy chains. It roared past a dejected and disqualified entry parked in a side yard. "That truck was kicked out of the parade because of what it said, I reckon," explained an observer. "Hellbound" was blazoned on its side.

Amid the entourage of burning oil and roaring engines rolled a sports utility vehicle carrying Miss Seafood Festival. "I thought we could get her into a boom truck," said Reverend Carpenter. "But the locals said, 'This is Miss Seafood Festival! We're not going to put her in a boom truck. We will get her a nice car.'" Accustomed to the carefully orchestrated North Carolina Seafood Festival in Morehead City, the tiara-crowned beauty smiled stiffly, unable to conceal her wariness over this unconventional escort through the marshlands.

The parade was over in a matter of minutes. A wake of diesel fumes, mingled with the smell of spray paint, hung over the crowd. "Last year we got here late and missed the parade," said Brenda Pigott, whose husband Crawford had died in the fall of '96 while at the wheel of his trawler *Bay Rambler*. "This year I made sure to be here on time. I don't want to miss out on the deer meat, although I never have cared for duck stew with rutabagas." She joined the rest of the spectators at the Cedar Island Community Center, where a feast of roast pig, venison, wild duck, clam chowder, and oysters awaited.

After the judging, with prizes awarded and all bellies full, Reverend Carpenter sat at a picnic table staring at the second piece of cake an elderly woman had brought him. The flotilla of boom trucks sat quietly in the gravel parking lot, decorations drooping and cooling engines ticking as their day of glory wound down.

"Oh Lord," Carpenter groaned.

"I'll take that cake if you don't want it," said seventeen-year-old Charles Garner. Garner was jazzed from winning "worst in show" for his skeleton of a jalopy held together by rust, rope, warning signs, and day-glow paint. "This is only the second year I've entered," said Garner, a clammer's son and himself a seasoned fisherman. "Winning worst ain't bad." He proudly showed off his plaque engraved with a poem:

> Lord, thank you for this wrecked old truck
> The scratches and dents bring me good luck
> The boom in the sky is a source of my pride
> As me and my truck keep watch o'er the tide
> We all know my truck ain't what it was, Lord
> The sad day is coming when it won't start
> The boom I will move to adorn my wife's Ford
> But no dumb car is comin' close to my heart.

Reverend Carpenter slid his slice of cake down to the kid. Now that the festivities were over, the minister's boyish face looked tired. It had been a tough year. Not content to stay within the quiet confines of his island congregation, Carpenter had begun testifying at fisheries hearings. One year earlier he had accompanied busloads of families to the capital city of Raleigh for the biggest protest march in anyone's memory. To Down East fishermen, who put a lot of stock in faith and prayer, the Reverend was nothing short of a gift from God. But Carpenter, newly baptized in the fiendish fires of fish politics, was not so sure.

"In my eighteen years of ministry, I have never seen anything to match what the government has been doing to small-scale commercial fishermen," he reflected. The preacher looked out over the thinning group—men in work boots, kids racing around trees, women chatting and smoking cigarettes. Cedar Island was one of a whole constellation of tiny Carolina fishing towns tucked into the marshes and behind beaches, shining small and steady amid the ever-changing push and pull of resort cities and high-dollar developments. Carpenter worried about the future of places like Cedar Island, full of people who didn't ask a lot of the world and who found heaven in a boom truck.

"I feel," Carpenter said, waving to a departing member of his congregation, "like a witness to a killing."

"Winning worst ain't bad," Charles Garner.
Photo by B. Garrity-Blake

"Why are people with nothing the problem?" "Clammer Bob" Worthington on Carrot Island.
Photo by B. Garrity-Blake

A Simple
Clammer

"Clammer Bob" Worthington's home was a black concrete sailboat anchored in Taylor's Creek in Beaufort. The *Hardrock* looked like an embattled pirate ship and had lost its mast long ago. Bob rowed his dingy the short distance to Carrot Island, part of the Rachel Carson Estuarine Sanctuary and one of the few barrier islands still harboring herds of wild ponies. He and his cat Kitten hiked along the horse trails, past snarling tangles of Smilax vines, yaupon bushes, and cedar trees. They emerged from the thicket to his favorite clamming grounds on the other side of the island, facing Shackelford Banks. The head of Bob's clam rake was made of several butter knives welded in a row. The rake cut thin, even lines in the wet sand, the tines glinting in the sun and clinking against the occasional clam.

"I rode on one of the buses to Raleigh that February," he recalled, placing the small gray bivalves in a bucket between Kitten's paws, as she liked to stand astride the rim to keep off the damp sand. Bob harvested the common hard clam, *Mercenaria mercenaria*, and sought the valuable one-inch-sized littlenecks. "The only thing the legislators did for us was let Reverend Carpenter open the meeting with a prayer." He glanced over at four bay ponies that had emerged from the woven canopy to graze on cord grass. "I don't think those politicians realized what it took for some of us just to get there," he reflected. "I was up by three a.m., and had to wade from my boat in Nasty Harbor to my bike. Do you remember how cold it was that morning? It snowed that day! I rode my bicycle over the Gallant's channel bridge, through Beaufort all the way to that grocery store parking lot where the buses were waiting."

Clammer Bob strove to keep life as simple as the hard-boiled egg and Mason jar of water he carried for his lunch. But the complications of modern society caught up with him one day after an encounter with two marine patrol officers. The officers had approached him as he and Kitten walked along the shoreline. The cat darted into the brush. Bob poured his clams onto the wet sand when the officers asked to count them. "Mr. Worthington," they informed him, "you are fifty-seven clams over the personal consumption limit. Where's your commercial tag?"

Clammer Bob explained that he had forgotten to attach the tag to his bucket. The patrolmen asked for identification, but became suspicious when the fisherman offered a photo card that was homemade. When Bob turned to put his wallet back in his pocket, one patrolman misunderstood his gesture and reached for the pepper spray. This led to a beach chase during which an officer pulled a gun on Bob, and the clammer almost drowned after his boots filled with water. Finally, with Coast Guard backup and a marine patrol helicopter thumping overhead, Clammer Bob was shoved down onto the beach and pepper-sprayed. He was handcuffed, transported across the creek to the Beaufort waterfront, and hauled to jail as outside diners at a trendy new-American-cuisine cafe applauded.

"The state nailed me, almost drowned me, because my paperwork was out of order," Bob said. "They violated me and stuck a gun in my face over a missing ten-cent clam tag. Well, I say that legislators and their so-called reform package—*their* paperwork is out of order! Nobody's pepper spraying *them*. When I heard about that march in Raleigh I signed on. You better believe I got on that protest bus."

The reform package was a complex set of recommendations that would, among other things, cap the number of commercial fishermen in North Carolina. During its three-year development, policymakers had declared a moratorium whereby no new commercial fishermen would be welcomed in the state. "They started out saying it's all about the environment, but ended up targeting fishermen," Clammer Bob declared. "Why are people with nothing the problem?" He put his rake down and nervously fingered an unlit cigarette. "I'll tell you why. Because we are of no economy to the system."

Fishermen had indeed become the center of attention during the overhaul of fisheries management. "If there's one thing I hope we get out of this process, it's the definition of a commercial fisherman," said Bob Lucas, attorney, angler, and avid fundraiser for the successful political campaigns of Governor James B. Hunt. The governor had rewarded Lucas, whose career in the courtroom had honed an impatient confidence that he could convince anybody of anything, with chairmanship of the Marine Fisheries Commission. The commission, charged with making fisheries rules for the state, included sport fishermen, commercial fishermen, and scientists. The commercial fishing community was loath to trust the leadership of a chairman who was both a lawyer and a sportsman, and Lucas found his patience put to the test.

"We want to create a class of professionals," Lucas continued enthusiastically, addressing a small group of men and women on Harkers
Island. But the folks assembled weren't so sure that the growing interest
in their occupation was benevolent. Fishermen knew they were already
professionals, and feared that the state's efforts to "find" and "define"
them would turn into a search and destroy mission. As soon as they
heard that the reforms were up for debate in the legislative building,
fishermen mobilized.

"So there we were, on the bus to Raleigh, and I still had on my
boots!" recalled Clammer Bob. "I forgot to bring shoes." He wasn't the
only protester wearing white rubber boots. Some wore Helly-Hansen
jackets, insulated winter jumpsuits fondly called "full goodies" by fishermen, and caps advertising Osprey-brand crab-pot line or Harris' Net
Shop in Atlantic. Men, women, and children poured off the buses, carrying signs that read "NO NET BAN" and "NO REFORM." The protesters received honks and waves of approval from urban passersby glad
to see any kind of collective disapproval on the staid streets of downtown
Raleigh.

Legislators and committee members were mystified by the protest.
Why would anyone object to fisheries reform? "Because these people are
scared for their lives," explained Sandra Kellum, whose husband Larry
fished in both the Carolinas. Nothing frightened fishermen more than
the possibility of a statewide ban on fishing nets, an issue running neck
and-neck with the reform bill through legislative halls. In 1995
Representative Billy Richardson of Fayetteville had introduced a bill,
based on his inability to catch a croaker in Pamlico Sound and the mis-
guided claim that fishermen were free to trawl waters 365 days a year,
to gauge public support for outlawing nets. It was rumored that the
Coastal Conservation Association, a sportfishing organization known
nationally for lobbying against the use of commercial fishing nets, was
behind the net-ban bill. Commercial fishermen saw the CCA as little
more than a wolf in sheep's clothing, wealthy sportsmen trying to gob-
ble up the resources for themselves while disguised as environmentalists.

"The Coastal Conservation Association can deny their involvement
with the net-ban bill all they want," said Hatteras fisherman Rob West,
who travelled to Raleigh with other Dare County fishermen to the press
conference where Richardson unveiled his bill. "But explain this to me:
We didn't have a copy of the bill. Heck, even the legislators from coastal
counties hadn't seen the bill, but the president of the CCA was in front
of us and he had a copy. I asked him if I could see it, and he hugged it
to his chest and said no."

Sandra Kellum saw a big picture emerging with the CCA's involvement. "Throughout the history of this country, oppression by certain groups has dominated and controlled other groups unjustly," she wrote to the reform committee. "Now that we look back on these episodes in history, we see how awful they really

Public information papers at a Fisheries Commission meeting. Photo by B. Garrity-Blake

were, and we wonder what type of leadership and what type of mentality allowed this to occur. We as a people lament our past mistakes and wish we could change history. Please do not allow the results of your actions and decisions to go down in infamy."

By the time the Raleigh meeting rolled around and committee members were set to vote, fishermen saw the threat of a net ban and the reform effort as two sides of the same coin. "If we don't pass this reform package," Bob Lucas had warned again and again, "you can expect a net ban." And in 1997 Representative Frank Mitchell, a poultry farmer from Iredell County, introduced another net-ban bill just as legislators were taking a look at the reform package; the lesser-of-two-evils approach in selling reforms to fishermen couldn't have backfired much more.

"The protest in Raleigh was the best show of solidarity the fishermen ever had," declared Clammer Bob. Fishing families from all along the coast lined up and slowly marched around the legislative block. They filed into the legislative building and filled the meeting chamber, joining the other public observers–a small knot of cheerfully attired sportsmen with their "Vote Yes to Reform" buttons pinned to pastel polo shirts and button-down Oxfords.

Even the children of fishermen seemed too large for the room of formality, decorum, and dark-suited legislators. The fishermen, with wind-burned faces and pale foreheads, stood in the back of the room with their caps in their hands, fingers tracking back and forth as though reading a message in the caps' felt. Lawmakers fidgeted with the proposals before them as an earsplitting silence fell over the room.

"That's when we asked if that preacher from Cedar Island could open the meeting with a prayer," recalled Clammer Bob. "So they went ahead and let him."

After Reverend Carpenter prayed, the deliberations began—albeit with awkwardness and hesitation. Until that morning, lawmakers had assumed that the public supported the proposal before them. They had heard support from the largest sportfishing club in North Carolina, as well as the only commercial fishing trade organization. Environmental groups supported the proposed reforms. No massive display of disapproval had been evident in a series of public meetings, except from the "Freedom Fighters," a group representing part-time fishermen who policymakers dismissed as hotheaded radicals.

"They felt us breathing down their necks, they saw our faces, and just couldn't approve the reform package that morning," said Clammer Bob. "But they only postponed the inevitable. They didn't have the guts to do it in front of us so they passed it later when the fuss died down." Citing an audit that showed the Division of Marine Fisheries to be in a state of disarray, the legislative committee postponed passing the reforms until the Division was running on track.

"Right after the meeting we got the runaround," Clammer Bob said, placing another clam in the bucket. "I talked to a legislator. She told me to go see so-and-so. I go see so-and-so and he tells me to go see the person I had already talked to! You get verbiage and no answers." He sighed.

"That was a long, cold day. I'm sure the people in Raleigh get plenty of money to be there: salary, per diem, mileage, who-knows-what-all. But me? When we got home to Beaufort, it was dark. Do you remember it snowed that night? We saw the flakes falling on the ride home. So I have to get on my bike, fifteen degrees outside, snow—ride back through Beaufort to Nasty Harbor. The tide was way high! I had to take off my boots and pants, and wade bare-assed to my boat. Walk across the deck leaving footprints in the snow. Got in my cabin and put a brick on my stove to try and warm up." He surveyed his half-full bucket of clams. Clean deep lines were raked all around him in the sand like a Zen tranquility garden.

"The legislators and policymakers and bureaucrats make like it's all so complicated," he said. "I say, quit pretending to be confused. There's nothing complicated about this—it's all about money. Does the simple clammer make himself clear?"

"I thank God and my parents for my stuff!" Lonnie Trinh at the Full Circle Crab Company. Photo by B. Garrity-Blake

La Casa de Jaiba

"So we're reformed! And we still have no limits on the number of crab pots," reflected crabber and armed-services veteran Willy Phillips. Phillips lived in Tyrrell County and ran his crab operation out of Fort Landing, on the banks of the Alligator River. The Alligator flows north into Albemarle Sound and cuts a broad swathe between Tyrrell and Dare Counties. "Fishermen just weren't ready for the concept of pot limits. And it didn't help that we were in the middle of a bonanza season when the plan was developed."

Phillips, looking like an organizer of the proletariat in fatigues, work boots, and free-flowing hair, fit well within the wilderness of sparsely populated and economically depressed Tyrrell County. But his rugged appearance belied his astute understanding of complex fisheries policy-making, an understanding that earned his appointment to the state's Marine Fisheries Commission. The crabber managed to traverse the worlds of rural fishing and urban development, never hesitating to speak his mind to people with high-paying desk jobs and expensive pleasure boats, or to those who lived hand to mouth. "I don't know anyone," said fisheries division director Pres Pate, "who has brought more integrity, dedication, and professionalism to the table than Willy Phillips." At the close of each commission meeting, Phillips chucked his giant stack of paperwork in the trash can before walking out the door.

"It all boils down to two camps," Phillips explained shortly before he finished his term on the commission. "There's those who believe we can fine-tune our control of nature, and there's those who still see some mystery in the world. I'd like to go on seeing that mystery." His appreciation of nature's secrets was shaped by life along the Alligator and Scuppernong Rivers, which spill into wide-open, salty Albemarle Sound and are bordered by endless swamp laurel, juniper trees, and scrub pine.

"Crabs are the basis for all other fisheries. What fish doesn't eat crab? And what fisherman around here doesn't depend on crabbing? That's why we came forward and said 'look, something has to be done.

We've got to get a handle on the numbers of pots and people.'" Phillips wiped his forehead and sat on a crate. "The whole reform effort started with the crabbers and ended with the crabbers. A few of us drafted a formula to limit pots, and in the end the fishermen balked at the idea when it was presented as part of a state plan. Seems their mistrust of the state outweighed their mistrust of each other!" He grinned. "Crabbers would rather deal with things themselves, without the government's help. But at least we got past all that hostility. I'm proud to say that as tense as things got around here, there was never any violence."

Phillips alluded to tensions that arose as a cultural transformation shook up the crab fishery. Generations of black women had long labored in the picking houses, until those with sore feet, bruised fingers, and aching backs broke the chain by pushing their daughters to seek other work. Latin American women filled the vacancies, and Mexican *cumbias* replaced gospel songs and Top 40 hits blaring from boom boxes.

La casa de jaiba is what Mexicans call the crab house. Processors throughout the state hired hundreds of Latinos in the 1990s under H-2 visas, ensuring that laborers would work for a single employer at a specified task without the option of quitting in favor of a better job in the United States. Women picked crabs and men cooked crabs, drove trucks, and even fished crab pots. Many spoke little or no English and would have suffered serious cultural vertigo were it not for the impressive network of friends and family established in *Carolina del Norte*.

This alien group of workers, along with an influx of Vietnamese fishermen, comprised the unwitting spark that ignited the firestorm of meetings, studies, and license freezes during the fisheries reform process that swept through the state. The Vietnamese community especially took root in the Albemarle Sound crabbing country, where today women in their homeland's traditional woven hats walk down main streets alongside farmers of Scots-Irish descent in bib overalls.

One hundred thirty-eight people signed a petition to Tyrrell County commissioners requesting an investigation into the "Importation of Non-Americans into Tyrrell County by Local Crab Company." A processing-plant owner, according to petitioners, was setting up Mexicans and Vietnamese "with boats, crab pots, and living quarters to work waters that the locals have worked for years." Reflecting the fears of those with few work options, the petition stated, "This operation will bust the industry that sustains the commercial fishing and crabbing community of the county."

The fear of a "hostile takeover" by non-American laborers was not limited to Tyrrell County. Processor John Henry Williams of Pamlico

County, who had hired four Mexicans, discovered that more than 4,000 of his pots were lost because someone had cut the lines. He and his Latino employees filed a lawsuit, charging that a group of crabbers conspired to eliminate Mexicans from the waters by vandalizing his operation and discouraging crabbers from selling to Williams Seafood.

The director of marine fisheries knew that the growing imbroglio had to be addressed. "The number of pots has tripled in the last six or seven years," he said, sidestepping any social, racist undertones to the conflict. "And why stop with crabs? Displaced fishermen could pour into North Carolina and create undue stress on the resources. Let's put a moratorium on *all* commercial licenses and revamp the fisheries management system."

What began as thinly veiled xenophobia in the remote areas of the Albemarle-Pamlico crab fishery grew to encompass every fisherman, every legislator, several new studies, hundreds of thousands of tax dollars, a plethora of newspaper articles and opinion pieces, public hearings and focus group meetings, and special interest groups.

"Let the big dogs stand. That's the position we took in the end—just open it up and let people crab their hearts out," reflected Phillips. "Some would discover they can't make it and the highliners would survive." Despite the rocky beginning, Phillips developed a good relationship with several of the Vietnamese crabbers. He and his wife Feather threw a Fourth of July party at his crab house and invited a mix of Anglo and Vietnamese fishermen. The Asian men showed up with their families and seemed to enjoy the American celebration complete with beer, barbeque, and a rock band.

"At one point a Vietnamese fella we call Shorty comes up to me and says, 'Willy, make speech!' I said, *'what?'* He says 'America two hundred twenty-four years old! Make speech!' I told Shorty I didn't think I could do it 'cause I'm not a great speechmaker and besides, I'm not always happy with this country. He says, 'This *great* country!'

"Shorty turns around and asks the electric guitar player to play 'God Bless America.' The guy shrugs and says he'll give it a try. Next thing I know Shorty's in some official posture, feet at a forty-five-degree angle, and he's singing 'God Bless America!' The Vietnamese congregate around him, all getting into this weird official position. Some are teary-eyed. And they all join in the song. The local boys just stop mid-swig, holding their beers, frozen." Phillips shook his head. "I got goose bumps. When Shorty finished, his family's hugging each other, crying, and then *they all leave*. They had been waiting for that point—to them, that was the whole point of Fourth of July. To us, it was just a day off work and an excuse to party. I said, 'Feather, we have witnessed something here today.'"

Phillips recounted this story while shaking a feisty tangle of crabs into baskets. The crabs, just unloaded by a crew of three Vietnamese men, sliced at the air with their claws. "Uh, oh," observed Phillips. "Here comes Lonnie and she doesn't look happy."

Lonnie Trinh was a Vietnamese woman who had hired the crew to fish her pots that day. She usually fished the 850 pots herself. After a short but pointed conversation in Vietnamese with her crew, Lonnie watched the men pull her boat from the dock and run it across the tiny harbor to its slip.

"I don't like that, Willy!" she told Phillips, joining him at the culling table. "I told him not to let that new guy drive my boat." Lonnie stood with her arms crossed, her left forearm scarred with slick patches from handmade tattoos she had burned off herself. A single mother of five, she had sent several children to college with her crabbing income. When not working the water she built crab pots for a local company for two dollars apiece. Lonnie was small but sturdy, and she looked younger than her forty-nine years. She glared out across the harbor. "I hire them and they should do what I ask them to do."

"Lonnie," Phillips said, shaking his head, "that's the nature of hiring a crew. You can't control everything from the hill. And your captain has a mountain of pots right there that he can set and crab himself. He's not exactly depending on your operation."

"Well, he can go ahead and set those pots! I don't need this. I can take care of my own stuff." Lonnie had lived in Tyrrell County for about eight years, getting into crabbing just when the petition began circulating. Phillips recalled that the work force of crabbers seemed to triple overnight when the Vietnamese entered the fishery. Locals were frightened at the implications and angry with the already unpopular fishhouse owner who had brought the Vietnamese into the area. But the Vietnamese crabbers worked themselves out from under the crab dealer, saving money to buy their own boats and pots. This garnered respect, and their relations with other crabbers improved. Phillips even helped Lonnie with the administrative red tape to secure her own commercial license.

"I'll fish my own pots tomorrow. I enjoy it! As long as I have my health and strength, and I thank God for that, I will keep crabbing." She tossed her head and examined the invoice Willy had handed her. "These guys say, 'oh, crabbing isn't for woman.' And you know what I tell them?"

Phillips laughed. "I can just imagine what you tell them, Lonnie."

Only a week before, Lonnie had gotten into an argument with her husband while they were working pots from their respective boats. He had been complaining over the airwaves to other fishermen about his wife, so Lonnie got on the radio and told him to shut up. When he threatened to ram her boat, she called the Coast Guard. By the time they got back to the dock, where they were met by local police, highway patrol, and marine fisheries officers, they were shouting in Vietnamese, the Coast Guard was confused, and Phillips was flabbergasted when Lonnie's husband announced that he was taking up all his pots and going back to Vietnam. Two days later his pots were in a pile at the dock, but—to Phillips's amusement—he was fishing alongside Lonnie as crew on her boat.

"I tell them that I have what it takes to make it in this business," she said.

"So you tell 'em you have the right stuff," said Phillips.

"I thank God and my parents for my stuff!" Lonnie declared, holding her hands up in fists and turning her face into the sun.

Lonnie Trinh and Willy Phillips settling up, Full Circle Crab Company.
Photo by B. Garrity-Blake

Moving croakers to China at Moon Tillet Fish Company, Wanchese.
Photo by B. Garrity-Blake

This
Pirate

He drove out of Tyrrell on a lonely blacktop, bordered by swampy water, moss-bearded trees, and muddy banks. Road signs warned of crossing bears, red wolves, and deer. Turtles, appearing to be on sentry duty beneath their helmet shells, lined the ditches running parallel to the road. Unless travelers made a special effort to reach the far-flung villages of Gum Neck, Kilkenny, Frying Pan Landing, or the county seat of Columbia, they encountered few signs of human habitation. Willy Phillips liked it that way. The wilderness of Tyrrell County was a sanctuary compared to his booming hometown of Wilmington.

Phillips passed the backside of the "Welcome to Tyrrell County" sign, but he knew it by heart. It read, "Our state senator is Marc Basnight and we're proud of it!" Tyrrell, Dare, and nine other waterborne counties formed North Carolina's first senatorial district, and they were represented by a Roanoke Islander who, according to the Center for Public Policy, was the most powerful politician in North Carolina. Few guessed that the kid from the coast entering the political arena in 1977 with no more than a high school degree would come to be senator pro tempore. "Everyone I talked to," Senator Melvin Daniels told a reporter, "said, 'I don't think he'll wear shoes. He'll show up barefoot!'"

Marc Basnight, when not in Raleigh, could be found pouring iced tea for after-church patrons at his family's restaurant on the causeway between Manteo and Nags Head. One foot in tourism and development, one foot in the seafood industry, and a fist around the purse strings of North Carolina's state government, Basnight literally worked the corner of his beloved state. He made no apologies for his pet local projects, including a million-dollar bike path on Roanoke Island and the replica of the Lost Colony's *Elizabeth II*, believing it only fair that his long-neglected northeast district receive its fair share. "Perhaps the N&O does not want anyone from eastern North Carolina serving in a position such as mine," he wrote, after the Raleigh *News and Observer* published a story accusing the senator of personally obstructing the enforcement of fishery laws in his district. "I truly believe they have been unfair to our people–be it farmer, universities, the highway system, or public education facilities. I question their opinions of those of us who reside in the East."

Phillips drove his pickup east across the long, flat, two-lane Alligator River bridge. It was a clear June morning, and the water had a slight chop. The road led to Dare County, where another bridge carried Phillips over Croatan Sound to Roanoke Island and Basnight's hometown of Manteo. Phillips passed manicured rows of crepe myrtles that bordered U.S. highway 64, shading sidewalks filled with bicycles and joggers. He made the short journey through the historical and pricey town of Manteo, and then embarked on the causeway and bridge to Whalebone Junction and the Outer Banks beaches of Nags Head and Kitty Hawk.

At a Nags Head motel Phillips took a seat among the eight other fisheries commissioners, joking "the best thing about a two-day meeting in Nags Head is I get to go home every night and sleep in my own bed."

Chairman Jimmy Johnson brought the meeting to order and said, "First on the agenda is public comment. If you have anything that you'd like to share with us, please step up to the microphone and state your name." Fishermen shifted uncomfortably in the windowless, temperature-controlled environment where biologists would give Power Point presentations full of numbers, facts, and certainty. Stepping before a podium is quite a reach for the windburned workers who feel at home among fish guts and cable grease on a boat, where everything is swinging and nothing is for certain.

The world of fisheries politics is small, and the eight or nine people who addressed the commission were familiar faces. But none was so familiar as the last–Willie Etheridge from Wanchese. Wanchese is a thriving fishing village hidden deep in the Roanoke Island marshes between the exploding tourist hotspots of Manteo and Nags Head. Etheridge was one of three heavyweight seafood dealers from Wanchese, all of whom knew how to rope and ride the international market like broncobusters.

Etheridge knew what was caught daily from the North Atlantic to the South China Sea. He carried a fat wallet stuffed with large bills. A bear of a man, Etheridge liked the company of fishermen and invited them to join him for dinner and drinks after meetings. When the time came to divvy up the tab, he'd shake his head and with unusual brevity say, "All taken care of." Fishermen might complain about the prices Etheridge paid for their fish but no one ever said he wasn't a generous man. One night in New York he took a long look at the band of Dare

County gill-netters gathered in a hotel lounge, exhausted after sitting all day observing a grueling fish politics meeting. "You ever been to Fulton Fish Market?" Etheridge asked the fishermen, knowing full well that some of them had never been to New York before. "Meet me in the lobby at three." Puffy-faced gill-netters spilled into the lobby in the dark of the night. A chauffeur waved them into a gaudy white stretch-limousine and whisked the fishermen through the city to the fish market where gruff fishmongers asked, "Wha'da sell to Avon Seafood? Yeh, we get good fish from down there."

Etheridge had sun-bleached hair, fists like conchs, and a face that turned to stone when he listened to bureaucrats talk about fish.

"If my voice sounds harsh," he started, standing before the commissioners sitting comfortably in the Nags Head conference room, "it's because I'm going to tell you what's happening to Etheridge Seafood in the year 2000." Willie Etheridge had taken the helm of Etheridge Seafood from his father, just like Joey Daniels took the helm of Wanchese Seafood from his father and Billy Carl Tillet took the helm of Moon Tillet Fish Company from *his* father. These Southern men, called "boys" by Wanchese old-timers, referred to their fathers as "Daddy." But thanks to the business-smarts of these dealers, with vessels plying the seas from Alaska to Venezuela, a triggerfish caught off Georgia found itself in New York's Fulton Market before its eyes had a chance to glaze over.

"Our business brought in close to ten million dollars last year," Willie Etheridge declared in a booming voice befitting a radio broadcaster. "*Ten million* to Dare County from our fish house alone." Even amid the high-dollar brilliance of Outer Banks tourism, an annual ten million bucks from one village seafood company is noteworthy.

"Yet," Etheridge emphasized to commissioners, "we are treated like criminals." Dogfish, monkfish, fluke, and swordfish–he recited a litany of fisheries that had been his bread and butter, but were now so parceled-out, divvied-up, and roped-off by recent rules and regulations that it was hardly worth fueling up vessels.

"If you would just research the motive behind many of the closures we face, you'd see how it really is," implored Etheridge, holding up a book as if it were the Bible. It was *Wetland Riders* by reporter Robert Fritchey, about the "con" in angler conservation efforts, the marine recreational corporations that bankroll them, and the Texas oilmen who started it all. "I bought several of these books and I'll be glad to give them out."

The commissioners were familiar with Etheridge, not only because he attended meetings faithfully, but also because he'd been involved in some high-profile fisheries disputes. Few received more publicity than "the tuna incident," a story that fast became legendary up and down the Carolina coast.

Captain Tom Fox, running the longline vessel *Triple Anthonys* out of Massachusetts, had radioed Etheridge and said he was coming in to pack out. It was the end of a twelve-day trip and Fox was exhausted. "Look, I got a monster of a bluefin off Virginia," he told Etheridge. "I'm guessing at least a thousand pounds. I gotta buyer meeting me."

"I gotcha! We'll be waiting for you," Etheridge responded. Prized by sushi and sashimi connoisseurs, bluefin tuna brought as much as forty dollars per pound. Fox's buyer specialized in grading tuna for the very discriminating Japanese market.

Lieutenant Fred Swain, from the state marine patrol, was on the docks when the boat arrived. Swain boarded the *Triple Anthonys* and, like everyone else in the harbor that day, commented on the size of the fish. Tom Fox, his T-shirt stained in perspiration and fish slime, stopped Swain and said, "Willie's guys are getting ready to pack me out. There's no problem, right?" It was difficult to keep on top of frequently changing state regulations, let alone federal regulations dictated by a global body called the International Convention for the Conservation of Atlantic Tuna.

"Let me check on that, cap'n," replied Swain. He telephoned Special Agent Jeff Radonski at the National Marine Fisheries Service in Beaufort while Etheridge's crew went to work unloading Fox's catch.

"Tell Etheridge and the captain of that vessel," Radonski said evenly, "that we are seizing that fish. The tuna is property of the U.S. Government, and must remain where it is until we arrive."

"Here, you better tell him yourself," said Swain, calling Willie Etheridge over to the phone.

"Do not unload that tuna," Agent Radonski told a stunned Etheridge. "That fish is illegal."

"What? What the hell are you talking about?" panted Etheridge, sweating in the June heat. Radonski's words raised his temperature by more than a few degrees. The special agent explained that federal law had recently changed, and bluefin tuna could no longer be landed south of the line at thirty-six degrees north latitude. The new line lay just five miles north of Wanchese and placed the closest port in Hampton, Virginia.

"Radonski," fumed Etheridge, "I want you to fax me, quote me, show me in writing the law stating that this fish is illegal in Wanchese." The fish baron hung up and stood quietly for a moment, staring out over the marsh past the ghostly relics of long-abandoned trawlers and steamers. Lieutenant Swain stepped around coils of rope to deliver the bad news to Captain Fox, who dropped a shovel full of ice and spun toward the tuna. Before his eyes the half-ton jackpot fish turned into an albatross that could cost him not only the profits of twelve days at sea, but thousands of dollars in fines and attorney fees.

Three hours later, as the sun took on weight and color in the western sky, Special Agent Radonski and a team of armed marshals rode into town like federales of the Old West. Etheridge stood with his arms folded, prepared to watch events unfold.

Radonski wasted no time in directing a forklift operator to carry the tuna into Etheridge's freezer. The fish bobbed over the ends of the fork.

"Hold on just a minute," Etheridge exclaimed, one hand signaling the driver to stop. "Where do you think you're going with that fish?"

"This fish is the property of the U.S. government," Special Agent Radonski replied flatly. "We'll store it in the freezer until arrangements are made for its removal."

Etheridge was outraged. "Listen, you can have the tuna, but I'll be damned if I'll store it for you!" He took over the forklift controls and shifted the machine into reverse. "Shoot me if you have to!"

He pushed the throttle to full speed, bouncing in unison with the thousand-pound tuna as the forklift hit potholes and mud puddles. Etheridge beelined for the main drag, the only route in and out of Wanchese and, with a dull thud, plopped the fish down in the middle of the road. "This fish belongs to the U.S. government," Etheridge announced to a growing crowd of gawkers. "Getting it out of Wanchese is their problem."

The fish created quite a spectacle in Wanchese. Rumors of a giant tuna in the road spread fast, and everyone hurried to the scene to see the creature rotting in the summer heat. The fish blocked traffic until the highway patrol arrived and a wrecker hauled it off by the tail to its final destination—the county landfill.

The bigger the fish, the meaner the politics. Willie Etheridge was quick to point out to fisheries commissioners the disparity between the worlds of sportsmen and commercial fishermen. "We don't begrudge the big-game anglers their sport," said Etheridge. "But these tournaments are a high-stakes form of gambling, with millions of dollars in incentives for anglers to catch and kill overexploited billfish."

No billfish attracted sportsmen more than marlin. Anglers followed the fish's blue streak to the ends of the earth. Marlin inspired sportsmen of great means to spend millions of dollars on vessels, to pay entry fees higher than some commercial fishermen's annual earnings, and to travel far and wide with hired captain and crew in search of the biggest and strongest. Marlin was Hemingway's fish, evoking the scent of fine bourbon and imported cigars, and the richness of a fishing story well told.

Since Hemingway's time, however, marlin has acquired a bigger and bigger payoff, growing to hundreds of thousands of dollars. At Morehead City's 43rd Annual Big Rock Blue Marlin Tournament, the winner bagged a 515.5-pound fish for a staggering grand prize of $942,100, more than the prize for the U.S. Open PGA Tournament that same year with the likes of Tiger Woods competing. The winning marlin was worth almost $2,000 a pound, a very lucrative fish for anglers whose manifesto is "we fish for sport, not profit."

"I am to be condemned if I kill a blue marlin by accident," wrote commercial fisherman Jeff Oden, pointing out that these billfish, off-limits to commercial fishermen since 1989 in the name of conservation, had a hefty bounty on their heads during sport-fishing tournaments. "Yet an angler is to be congratulated and rewarded if he kills one for the fun of it."

Most billfish, after a long, arduous fight, are pulled aboard, tagged, and released back into the water in hopes that they will survive. The largest marlin, however, are killed. The victors, with deep tans and Hawaiian print shirts, pose amid a throng of spectators next to the fish hanging by its tail.

The Big Rock Blue Marlin Tournament, whose charitable donations each year are highly praised and publicized, came under fire when a newspaper revealed what happened to the giant fish after the photo-op was over and the crowd went home. Promoters had claimed that all fish were shipped to the Virginia Institute of Marine Science for research purposes. Dr. John Graves, the lead marlin researcher at VIMS, told a different story. He had sent a technician to Morehead for the 1992 tournament, but got little cooperation. "It didn't seem like tournament officials were very interested in science," Graves explained. "They didn't want us touching the fish at the dock. They just wanted someone to take the fish away."

The marlin were unceremoniously trucked to a local landfill and buried after their beaks were sawed off for the taxidermist. Photos of the trashed fish fell into the hands of a commercial fisherman, who made T-shirts reading "Sportfishing Conservation–Only in America" next to a depiction of the mutilated marlin in a dumpster. The T-shirt, like Fritchey's book on the political power of angler organizations, makes occasional appearances at public hearings, as frustrated watermen and fish dealers place their last chip on the power of truth and evidence.

"You look at the commercial fishing industry like we are a bunch of pirates," declared Willie Etheridge, wrapping up his assessment of the seafood industry in the new millennium.

"This pirate," Etheridge said, pausing to scan the faces of the nine policymakers before him, "*this* pirate has produced enough seafood in the last year and a half to feed every American citizen at least one mess of fish. I am proud of that. And you people ought to be proud of it too."

Avon Seafood, Hatteras Island.
Photo by Susan West

Miss Blue canning "Chowan's Best" at Perry-Wynns Fish Company.
Photo by B. Garrity-Blake

Red
Herring

"We have been approached–the first of this kind–by a group of fishermen, the Byrum brothers on the Chowan River, asking us to buy their nets, and to buy their boats, and to put them out of business," Marc Basnight told fellow senators as debate on the Fisheries Reform Act wound toward a close in 1997. "And, that there be no past, and that there be a different future, and that we take them off the water forevermore." The Byrum brothers were pound-netters, who carried on the historical practice of scooping live fish out of "pounds," which are large heart-shaped corrals of net held in place by sapling trunks. They set their pounds in the Chowan River for the spring herring runs.

Curving north in scorpion-tail fashion from the great Albemarle Sound, the Chowan River cuts through the uppermost region of what some North Carolinians might call the boondocks or no man's land. Writer Bland Simpson proudly calls it Sound Country, where "rivers go sliding off into swamps and gliding by grand bluffs, ancient forests drown slowly in the rotting shred of peat in baylands and pocosins, new grasses green up each spring in marshes both saltwater and fresh." It is also a region that has sustained scattered, fishery-dependent hamlets for centuries.

"I believe that there's four pound-net fishermen left fishing for herring on the Chowan River," Basnight continued. "They told me that herring landings reached a peak of 19,000,000 pounds, down to just 400,000 pounds today. To say that this was caused by the commercial fishermen on the Chowan River, with four of them left, or with the six or eight or ten or twelve that were there just a few years ago, is just not so."

The beauty and solitude of the Indian-named Chowan, Perquimans, and Pasquotank Rivers have turned more than one writer to poetry. But there was nothing poetic about the frightening description of the Albemarle found in a 1998 University of North Carolina-Wilmington report entitled "Sediment Contamination in North Carolina's Estuaries."

"Albemarle Sound was the most contaminant enriched region in

North Carolina," the report read, with "lead, mercury, zinc, nickel, chromium, DDT and PCBs." The scorpion tail of the Chowan, thanks to urban waste, industrial chemicals, and agricultural runoff, had acquired a poisonous sting.

Basnight's speech to the North Carolina Senate reached an emotional crescendo. "The Byrum Brothers and others have been told to remove their nets. They were blamed for something neither they, nor their families before them, did. We always hear that there's not enough data to effectively manage our fisheries. Yet we always come back to the same old fisherman and tell him that he is the culprit, he is the problem, he is the villain, that he is the one destroying our fish for recreational fishermen."

"I never dreamed it would come to this," said the owner of a fish-packing house in Edenton. "It used to be we couldn't handle all the herring that came through here. We shipped them all over the world."

Herring is the granddaddy of commercial fisheries in North Carolina. Eighteenth-century planters orchestrated the strong backs and worn hands of slaves, along with indentured and hired labor, to work mile-long seine nets from the riverbanks, and to cut and salt the catch. Later, horses and then steam engines replaced slaves for hauling the huge nets. "During the season of 1880 there were eleven large seines in operation at the head of the sound," wrote a nineteenth-century investigator in G.B. Goode's federal fishery report. "In addition, a number of smaller seines were operated, the seine fisheries on the Chowan extending a short distance about the junction of the Notaway and the Meherrin."

Alewife and blueback herring spend most of their adult life in the Atlantic Ocean, but they migrate to sluggish freshwater rivers each spring to spawn. The arrival of spring in the Albemarle is announced not by the gentle faces of daffodils but by swirling runs of pure aquatic muscle, moving up the sound's veins of the Chowan, Meherrin, Pasquotank, Roanoke, and Perquimans. Records kept from 1835 to 1874 by the Willow Branch Fishery Company, located at the head of the Chowan, show that the timing of the herring and shad arrival was like clockwork, varying only by a day or so year after year.

"Used to be like a circus out here, each spring. Weren't nothing on Easter weekend to see five, six hundred people out here, all buying and selling fish," said pound-netter Herbert Byrum. The Byrum brothers sold their catch to Perry-Wynns Fish Company, the world's largest supplier of salted and pickled herring. Every spring, workers spilled down the hill in the town of Colerain to the rickety wooden wharfs and cavernous warehouses and canning rooms on the banks of the Chowan.

Black and white, young and old, worked together, heaving baskets of herring out of wide-bodied, shallow boats. Women expertly cut, salted, and packed the fish. Anyone who wanted to work had a job during herring season.

Perry-Wynns still packages Chowan-brand salt-cured herring fillets. "Old time taste for a new generation" is their slogan, promoting a ready-to-cook herring product not requiring the traditional lengthy soak time. The big-money product, a much-sought-after delicacy since the inception of the herring fishery, is the roe, and Perry-Wynns cans "Chowan's Best." But "Chowan's Best" is no longer a domestic product—the roe herring is shipped in from Canada.

"Pollution took the biggest part of the industry," reflected Herbert Byrum. "But pollution is not the whole story of the herring's demise. Overfishing did the rest." Byrum referred not to the estuarine pound-net crews, but to the fleets of for-

Salting herring at Perry-Wynns Fish Company. Photo by B. Garrity-Blake

eign factory trawlers that appeared along U.S. shores in the 1950s. The foreign ships were capable of catching, processing, and freezing huge quantities of herring. William H. Warner traced the development of factory trawler fleets from the Soviet Union, Germany, Poland, and Spain in his book, *Distant Water: The Fate of the North Atlantic Fisherman*. Scouting ships "took the pulse" of waters, and big fleets were then called in to harvest, load, and process massive concentrations of fish.

"I remember flying surveillance out of North Carolina in the winter of '68, flat-hatting in a Grumman 'Goat' three hundred feet above the water," recollected a National Marine Fisheries Service enforcement official. He told Warner, "You could count as many as two hundred

Communist-bloc trawlers within a twenty-mile area off Hatteras Island. Every one of them would be wallowing–filled to the gunwales, you might say–with herring." The passage of the Fisheries Conservation and Management Act in 1976 expanded the United States' territorial waters to 200 miles off the coast. The first seizures of foreign vessels under the Act involved the over-harvest of river herring. But it seemed that the 1976 legislation, now called the Magnuson-Stevens Act, had come too late.

Faced with predictions of a herring stock collapse, the North Carolina Marine Fisheries Commission voted in 1995 to institute a short-ened herring season. Scientists estimated that the short season would reduce catches of herring by 70 percent. Watermen would have to stop fishing by April fifteenth, before the fish began their run back to the Atlantic. The fishermen's stitched tunnels would divert only a few errant herring to the heart of the pound before nets were gathered up for the year.

"I deplore the human tragedy that will result from closing this fish-ery for half of its season," said a Chapel Hill scientist serving on the fish commission. The scientist had little doubt that reduced water quality played a role in the decline of herring, but–considering the severity of the situation and the limited authority of the commission–he argued that the commission had to do *something*. "No one has ever told me that the world works in a way that's fair."

"Paper mill effluents kill all the nutrients the herring need," said Bobby Byrum, learning of the commission's ruling. "But the state won't regulate them or their waste. They just keep regulating fishermen right up the river and let the mills keep doing what they're doing."

The truncated season knocked the starch out of the pound-netters, who feared that their names would be on the last page of the final chap-ter of herring history. "The watermen would've agreed to a compromise closure of May first. But April fifteenth about puts them all out of busi-ness," explained a packinghouse owner. When the Byrum Brothers had to remove their nets from the water on the fifteenth, the 1995 run of her-ring had lasted only five days.

"We weren't even going to set nets this year, but this is all we've ever done. You can't just give up and die," said Bobby Byrum.

The Albemarle watermen are a tenacious lot, and none more so than Terry Pratt, president of the Albemarle Fishermen's Association. Pratt, his sunburned skin contrasting starkly with his white-blond hair, threw himself into salvaging the herring fishery. His worn work truck sat in the parking lot of the Legislative Office Building in Raleigh more than in his driveway in Merry Hill. Known for his unflagging promotion of "holistic fisheries management," Pratt talked herring with everyone from the governor to sport fishermen–he produced charts, statistics, photos, and video footage to support the watermen's case. He and his fellow fishermen hashed out an alternative management strategy.

"The Chowan River Pound-Net Fishermen," Pratt wrote in a letter to the state's fisheries director, "with the exception of one, will agree to remove one-half of all their registered pound net sets if the Division of Marine Fisheries would extend the Herring Fishing Season until May tenth." The offer to reduce the number of pound nets by 50 percent was no token gesture.

"Bring fishermen on board in a joint effort to preserve our resources," implored Lee Wynns of Perry-Wynns Fish Company. "The fisherman is a keen observer with a wealth of knowledge to share if given a chance. *Work* with fishermen." The Marine Fisheries Commission agreed, and accepted the Albemarle watermen's management concept of less nets in lieu of a shortened fishing season. Although the details still needed to be ironed out, the fishermen allowed themselves to believe that their input was taken seriously in the management of herring. "I think that this is what fisheries management is all about," confirmed the commission chairman. Not everyone was pleased with the decision, however. The director of the Coastal Conservation Association, a recreational fishing organization, complained that the agreement "smacks of backroom deals."

The illusion of cooperation between fishermen and managers evaporated quicker than morning mist on the river. Albemarle watermen received a letter from the fisheries director, who seemed to be working independently of his commission, making it clear that he had his own idea of what to implement–an annual quota of herring. The fishermen were stunned. In all the meetings with state officials, a harvest quota had never been brought up. The fisheries director, newly transplanted from New Jersey, had earned the nickname "The Phantom" because he was often absent from his office, didn't return phone calls, and avoided contact with fishermen. A paltry understanding of the herring fishermen was painfully obvious in his letter, which concluded "the success in this effort may serve as a test of the effectiveness of such joint government-citizen management ventures in the future."

"This is the straw that broke the camel's back," said a Chowan River fisherman. "This so-called compromise. I don't think you'll find a commercial fisherman around the Albemarle area who's willing to work with those state biologists any more." "The Phantom" resigned after snowballing complaints and criticisms, and a new director, Preston Pate, was sworn in the same week that the 1997 Fisheries Reform Act became law. He inherited the task of overseeing a new herring management plan in the troubled wake of his predecessor.

Jamesville is a speck on the map in the midst of Carolina Sound

"When you tell them there ain't no herring, they say 'what?' " J. G. Layton, Layton's Landing. Photo by B. Garrity-Blake

Country, where people are content to pass spring evenings down at the Cypress Grill along the slow-moving Roanoke River, eating fresh fried herring, bones and all. Jamesville hosts the spring Herring Festival, a rite of renewal and celebration for the townsfolk. "The Herring Festival is a longstanding tradition, a time of homecoming and a source of pride to the citizens of Martin County and the town of Jamesville," resolved Martin County commissioners in March 2000, shortly after a 300,000-pound quota was enacted as part of the new herring fisheries management plan. Organizers of the Jamesville Herring Festival feared that the quota would be reached well before their Easter Monday celebration. Town officials requested that fisheries director Preston Pate set aside a portion of the quota for the weekend of the festival. "Martin County is an economically distressed county. The Herring Festival not only brings dollars to our local fire departments and other nonprofits, but it provides a much-needed lifting of our community spirit."

The humble resolution from Martin County underscored one of countless small injuries that can result from a stroke of the management pen; unforseen during the debates, minuscule and unimportant to some, but critical to the cultural fabric of small places. Director Pate, with the Marine Fisheries Commission's blessing, complied with their request.

Just north of Jamesville, fish-house owner J.G. Layton was also fretting over the new quota. He stood mending a net at Layton Landing, a small cove along the Cashoke River that fed into the Chowan. Four small wooden buildings stood in pairs over the sleepy river. Several workboats, including Terry Pratt's, dozed at the docks. The water was covered in slow-moving swirls of yellow pine pollen. "Easter season, everyone has a fish fry," reflected Layton. "All the churches have their homecomings, and fried herring has always been a part of that around here." The biggest building at Layton Landing was a weathered fish house full of coolers, nets, foul weather slickers, and boots. Over the door was a ghost of a sign, a faded outline of a fish and the word "Layton" barely legible. The sign was made by J.G. Layton's father and had been there as long as J.G. could remember.

"Thing is, a lot of black folks from New York and other cities show up every spring for homecoming–they come here with coolers so they can bring herring home. They grew up eating herring. They want their kids to taste it. They want to serve it to their friends up north and say, 'This is where we came from.' When you tell them there ain't no herring, they say, 'What?'"

Layton looked up from his mending as a car pulled up and three women and a man got out. "Got any herring today?" one of the women asked.

"Not since seven thirty, eight o'clock this morning," Layton answered. "Got some other, though." He looped his large plastic needle through the mesh and led the group to the fish house. They peered into his coolers of fish, one brimming with catfish bigger than baseball bats, and settled on some perch.

"Yeah, it was a slap in the face when we got the quota and Nucor got the permits," Layton said, resuming his mending. Nucor Steel Company was building a steel recycling plant on a 990-acre site along the banks of the Chowan near Tunis. The Marine Fisheries Commission raised concerns about the environmental impact of the project, spelling out the hazards of industrial waste, watershed integrity, dock turbidity, and barge traffic. But despite objections from one of its own agencies, the Hunt administration successfully enticed the corporation to build on the banks of the Chowan with tax credits of $116 million.

"While we share the Commission's concern for the status of the herring stock, we have not seen information that demonstrates any reasonable potential for the Nucor project to have a significant adverse impact on the fishery," explained a letter from the Department of Health and Natural Resources. "There is evidence of a severely over-fished stock with continued harvest on the small brood stock. Until that condition is remedied, we find it difficult to conclude that a project as carefully and closely regulated as Nucor's could have so adverse an impact." Senator Basnight's assertion that the few remaining pound-net crews served as a red herring to divert attention from environmental improprieties never rang truer.

"They're building that plant right now as hard as they can go," said J.G. Layton, pulling his mending needle through the net. "But a *double* slap in the face is that I went ahead and applied for a job there and they didn't call me." Residents of the rural Chowan region were discovering that Nucor was not quite the employment panacea they had hoped. Layton sighed. "It's just as well. Reckon they thought I was too old."

Cashoke Creek on the Chowan River.
Photo by B. Garrity-Blake

Preparing for a TED Protest.
Photo by B. Garrity-Blake

Turtle
Stew

"While browsing in a local store," wrote Harkers Islander Linda Gillikin to the editor of the *Carteret County News-Times*, "I overheard two women discussing how nicely beach nourishment was proceeding." Beach nourishment is the expensive and controversial method of pumping sand from the ocean bottom onto the shoreline to build up an eroding beach and protect expensive oceanfront homes. Two loggerhead and two Kemp's Ridley sea turtles had just been sucked up in the pump and killed, temporarily halting nourishment efforts along Pine Knoll Shores in Carteret County. "One woman stated, 'You know, if they catch one more turtle, they will have to stop dredging.' The other lady exclaimed, 'Oh, just kill it. What difference could one turtle make?'

"I was compelled to answer, 'Now you can understand how the fishermen feel.' The woman brushed by me as if I had not spoken, as if I was not standing there. I could not help but feel how the local fishermen do—unseen, unheard and voiceless. I was struck by the gross inequality that the woman's statement reflected."

Gillikin's one-sided encounter with the women in the store was yet another small incidence of cultural values colliding along the coast. The unique chords and harmonics of coastal life, shaping how villagers relate to the natural world, go unnoticed by new condominium owners intent on finding the perfect blue carpet to set off the slice of sea visible from their sunrooms.

Down East fishing families are only a generation or two removed from the days when sea turtles were marketed as a commodity. In an 1880 report published in G.B. Goode's *Fisheries and Fishery Industries of the U.S.*, Frederick True described an unusual method of turtle capture in Bogue Sound, the calm waters adjacent to today's Pine Knoll Shores where the beach nourishment controversy unfolded. Invented by Captain Joshua Lewis, "turtle diving" replaced spearing and yielded a live animal for market.

The fisherman "ties the painter of his boat to his leg and dives upon the turtle," wrote True. "Seizing the anterior edge of the carapace with one hand, and the posterior edge with the other, he turns the head of the turtle upward, so the animal immediately rises to the surface, bringing the fisherman with it." Steering the turtle "toward a shoaler spot" with his boat dragging behind him, the fisherman would gain footing in shallow water, seize the turtle, and heave it into the boat.

In 1987 the Harkers Island United Methodist Women put together a cookbook called *Island Born and Bred* that included a recipe for "Turkle." It called for one medium-sized loggerhead sea turtle, quartered. The meat should be parboiled, the recipe directed, and stewed with pork dripping, potatoes, onions, and flour dodgers. "Need 'old-timer' to cut turtle out of shell," the recipe reads, "not everyone can do it!" A disclaimer at the top of the page noted that the inclusion of the recipe was not meant to encourage illegal activity. Cordoned off in the "traditional" section of the cookbook alongside recipes for loons and robins, the turtle dish stirs up mixed thoughts of long-ago Sunday dinners and modern culinary crimes of a felonious nature.

Core Sounders who trawled for shrimp under the night skies were thinking hard about turtles at the time the Methodist Women's cookbook came out. Fishermen's attitudes toward sea turtles began to change in the late 1980s when U.S. shrimpers were blamed for the impending extinction of the ancient reptiles. In a cornerstone report dedicated to the "peaceful coexistence of sea turtles and shrimp fisheries," the National Academy of Sciences proclaimed that shrimping was responsible for 86 percent of all human-caused turtle mortalities. Downplaying the role of beachfront development, off-road vehicle traffic, pollution, and oil drilling, the report concluded "the incidental capture of sea turtles in shrimp trawls kills more turtles than all other human activities combined."

"What few turtles I've caught in my thirty years of fishing have been so lively they liked to tear my nets scrambling to get back in the water," said a Core Sounder, fingering a Sea Grant brochure that offered fishermen instructions on how to revive a sluggish turtle. "But hell, I'll give 'em mouth-to-mouth if it'll keep us from pulling turtle shooters!"

"Turtle shooters," known officially as Turtle Excluder Devices or TEDs, are round metal grids that Gulf Coast shrimpers had been required to use since 1979. TEDs are fitted into trawl nets. The bars of the grid are spaced wide enough to permit shrimp to pass through to the net's tailbag, but close enough to stop turtles and deflect them out through a flap in the net. Gulf fishermen, in high profile protests like the blocking of Galveston Bay, complained that too many shrimp escaped with the turtles, and that debris-clogged TEDs fouled up their harvests. "With turtle shooters, you ain't shrimping no more," agreed Tarheel fisherman Larry Kellum, who helped test TEDs in Atlantic Ocean waters. "You're just burning fuel and excluding turtles."

"Like it or not, TEDs are coming," a North Carolina Division of Marine Fisheries staffer said to the dozens of fishermen who met at the Marshallberg Volunteer Fire Department building. "National Marine Fisheries Service is going to require TEDs here and everywhere." The Center for Marine Conservation, an environmental organization head-quartered in Washington, D.C., had levied a lawsuit against National Marine Fisheries Service, charging that the agency was not upholding the Endangered Species Act by allowing some shrimpers to forgo the use of Turtle Excluder Devices. Such lawsuits against the federal government became common in the 1990s, prompting one environmental group's executive director to admit, "I do think litigation is overused. It's hard to identify what the strategic goal is, unless it is to significantly reshape society." The "reshaping of society" was precisely what Down East fishermen feared.

The Division of Marine Fisheries staffer shifted in his chair and adjusted his baseball cap, aware of the impact of his news. "From January on," he emphasized, "you have to be outfitted with TEDs or your boat will be seized, your catch impounded, and you'll be charged with a felony."

"The Bible says man shall hold dominion over all the creeping crawling things of this earth," said a thin, gray-haired fisherman as he stood and pointed to the bureaucrat. "The government is placing the value of a turtle above the value of a man's family. *That*, my friend, ain't right!"

"Sit down, Daddy," said his son, easing him back in the chair. "You know the government never did put no stock in the Holy Bible." But the old-timer voiced a concern felt by many in the Down East area—a reranking was afoot that not only put turtles above humans, but put working-class fishermen below everybody else. They asked why, in spite of the Endangered Species Act, beach homes and condominiums were erected on sandy barrier islands. Or why sport fishermen could still take four-wheel-drive trucks along National Park beaches that served as turtle nesting grounds. Fishermen sorely resented shouldering the burden of a new taboo unshared by the wider coastal community.

"The turtle watchers that want us gone live in those very condos and beach homes that destroyed the sand dunes and nesting grounds," said a fisherman from Salter Path. "But nobody wants to talk about that."

Linda Gillikin, reflecting on the shoppers' cavalier attitude toward the beach nourishment turtle deaths, agreed. "A turtle can be sacrificed to protect the valuable real estate of some, but not the precious livelihood of others," she wrote. "Surely the life of a turtle caught in the dredging of sand to protect one man's property has the same worth as a turtle caught in the net of a fishermen working to protect the life of his family."

"I am concerned about the financial and spiritual well-being of those fishing families I serve in Atlantic," wrote the Reverend Benjamin S. Sharpe of the Atlantic United Methodist Church. He referred to another regulation that infringed upon the religious sensibilities of some fishermen—a proposal to close Friday nights to trawling, which would shave off the last workday of the week before shrimping resumed Sunday evening at sundown. Many fishermen who had opted out of working Sunday night to be with family or go to church now felt compelled to start their week on the "Lord's Day" to make up for the loss of Friday night.

"Fishermen feel split between their Christian commitment and the need to provide for their families," the Reverend Sharpe continued. "The interests of commercial fishermen, recreational fishermen, and conservationists seem to be nearly mutually exclusive at times. Commercial fishing has been a part of Down East life since before 1684. Recent legislation and policy have hastened the erosion of the unique, traditional culture."

Twila Nelson, married to a Harkers Island fisherman, led the effort to retain Friday night shrimping. She belonged to the Harkers Island Grace Holiness Church and followed church doctrine by not cutting her hair, donning a skirt at all times, and going without a lot of makeup or jewelry. Her appearance belied a razor-sharp political sophistication—she later became a governor appointee to both the Marine Fisheries Commission and the Joint Legislative Commission on Seafood and Aquaculture. Nelson called a press conference on Harkers Island, and the fishermen's concerns hit the evening news. Nelson's leadership further awakened the political consciousness of fisher-women.

Women accustomed to mending nets, keeping accounts, filling out required state and federal fishery forms, driving fish trucks, and juggling a slew of other tasks simply added "taking on the government" to the list of chores necessary to keep the family business up and running. Twenty-two-year-old Tina Beacham explained, "Our husbands can't go to all these meetings. They're working all the time, trying to make a living. It's up to us to go to these meetings and fight." Women up and down the coast formed "ladies auxiliaries" to the North Carolina Fisheries Association, a trade group historically controlled by the "fish barons," a powerful group of seafood wholesalers.

"There is just this terrible sense of unease," explained Dorothy Dunn, co-organizer of the Hatteras-Ocracoke Auxiliary. Dunn reflected on the best thing that was rising out of the turtle conflict–fishing towns were coming together and women were laying the foundation for a statewide political network. "We all have an awareness that the world as we know it is about to change. We also know that we had better be prepared to understand and shape that change."

"Remember that we are on the Endangered Species list along with the turtle," wrote Beacham in an appeal for Carteret County women to organize. "Commercial fishermen need to pull together as one." Never before had fishermen's wives, let alone fishermen, been so visible in the public eye. It was a role few felt comfortable with, but everyone–even men who found themselves cooking supper and putting kids to bed while their wives attended meetings–understood its importance.

> *God grant that I may fish until my dying day;*
> *And when I come to my last cast, I'll then most humbly pray*
> *When in the Lord's safe landing net I'm peacefully asleep*
> *That in His mercy I'll be judged as good enough to keep.*

The "fisherman's prayer" opened each Carteret Auxiliary meeting. "The Feds are going to shove TEDs right down our throats," Auxiliary president Anita Darden declared to a room full of men and women. "I think it's time we got radical." One month later, she found herself heading a protest march to the National Marine Fisheries Service laboratory on Pivers Island in Beaufort. Although the laboratory housed scientists and not policymakers, the women understood that even the smallest protest would garner publicity, and could possibly subvert the workings of bureaucratic procedure.

"I hope my voice doesn't shake," said Darden. "I know I'll be nervous." On this cold March morning in 1993, a modest group of men and women gathered at a road leading to the NMFS building. Two fishermen, P.D. Mason of Bettie and Marshall "Skeeter" Saunders of Atlantic, stood stoically while women tied sections of fishing net to their bodies. The nets held round TED grids, and from a distance the men resembled turtles carrying their shells. The Auxiliary women passed out posters to the group, with slogans such as "COMMERCIAL FISHERMEN: THE ENDANGERED SPECIES" and "TOW TIMES, NOT TEDS."

The knot of protesters, bearing blue "Save the Commercial Fishermen" flags, and accompanied by a couple of reporters and a cameraman, walked down the road and stopped in front of the NMFS building. "I saw them coming that morning, and thought, oh no," a NMFS biologist recalled. "I slipped in a side door. All I could think was, poor Bud!" Ford "Bud" Cross, director of the Pivers Island laboratory, met the protesters in the front parking lot.

"My name is Anita Darden," blared the voice through the megaphone. "I am president of the NCFA Auxiliary Carteret County Chapter. My husband is a commercial fisherman. I think you know why we're here." A fourteen-year-old girl held a clipboard for Darden so she could read the statement. "We will not stand for irresponsible policies that wreck lives and shatter communities. We will not be unjustly labeled as turtle-killers. We are appalled at your senseless policies in an area with a depressed economy and no decent job alternatives." The March wind whipped her hair around. The reporter panned his camera around the shivering group. "How dare you burden us with this politically driven agenda without even pretending to study the consequences?" Director Bud Cross, an empathetic and soft-spoken man, listened intently. He understood that the protest was staged to attract attention to their cause.

"We are not ignorant fishwives and rednecks. We are hard-working human beings with children to raise, mortgages to meet, and dreams to live for. We have coexisted with turtles for generations. We demand evidence that we are destroying turtles. We demand respect as human beings and American taxpayers. We demand that you revoke this unfair TED policy before more damage is done." Darden took a wavering breath and finished up. "We demand the right to go on with our work

"We demand the right to go on with our work and quietly live our lives."
Photo by B. Garrity-Blake

and quietly live our lives."

On the six o'clock news, Anita Darden was shown delivering a stack of petitions containing some 2,000 signatures opposing the TED rule. The reporter conveyed that a small revolution was at hand. Before the evening was through, Andy Kemmerer from NMFS's southeast regional office in St. Petersburg, Florida, called Anita Darden. "What do you want me to do?" he inquired. Within days, Kemmerer flew to Carteret County to meet with Anita Darden, other Auxiliary members, and commercial fishing families numbering so many they filled the high school auditorium. The Auxiliary and fishermen presented maps and data supporting their objections, but Kemmerer made clear the NMFS bottom line: under the Endangered Species Act, the government had the power to eliminate trawling altogether in turtle-inhabited waters. In that light, he reasoned, were TEDs not a preferable alternative?

"We thought all we had to do was expose the facts," said Tina Beacham, sitting in No Name Pizza in Beaufort with several other fishermen's wives. They were licking their wounds after hearing the TEDs would go into effect despite their efforts. "We thought that once the truth was known, the knots would untangle and fairness would prevail."

"Yeah, apparently facts are beside the point," said Anita Darden, taking a long drag off her cigarette. "And it's not like we get to pack up and go home now. Just like those trick birthday candles—the fires are going to keep popping up. We run around trying to put out the flames, but there's absolutely no end to them."

"The more I thought about the conversation in the store about beach nourishment and the turtle deaths," reflected Linda Gillikin, "the more I realized the real issue is not about turtles. It is about an underlying lack of understanding and respect for people who for generations have lived and died in the waters of Carteret County.

"For us, the ocean is not simply for recreation, a lovely backdrop for entertaining in our beach homes. Our lives are intricately and fiercely interwoven with the water. Whether or not we still net our living from its dark depths as our grandparents did, each of us can look into the rolling waves and see the faces of loved ones who lived and died in the sting of its salty breath.

"No one would chose the hard life of commercial fishing for their sons. But even today, unbidden and undenied, the water chooses our sons. The living that they eke out is being strangled by regulations, requirements, and restrictions. The fishermen will be blamed for the extinction of the turtle. The reality is that both the turtle and the fisherman have been sold to the highest bidder."

"Mary's *still* digging scales out of the washer!" Kenny Lewis scaling mullets.
Photo by B. Garrity-Blake

The Mullet
Wrapper

"Here's tarter sauce and cocktail sauce for your oysters," Dorothy Dunn said to her four-top as a party of red-faced sport fishermen burst through Tides Restaurant's front door. The anglers brushed by her, pulled off their Gore-Tex jackets, and plopped down in captain's chairs at a corner table. Their voices boomed loudly as though still competing with the roar of the wind and the pounding surf.

Dorothy pulled the pen from behind her ear and walked over to the corner table. She and her husband Paul had sailed into Buxton harbor from Florida twenty years earlier, drawn to Cape Hatteras in search of the powerful, rolling swells famous with East Coast surfers. They figured they'd pick up whatever jobs they could find, surf until wanderlust struck again, and move on. The couple never imagined that twenty years later they'd be dyed-in-the-wool Cape Hatteras villagers–Dorothy taking an unexpected foray into politics and Paul struggling with the biggest career choice of his life.

Not long after sailing into Buxton, Paul landed a coveted position as a crewmember for Bob Swartz's pound-net operation. A Paul Bunyon-sized man whose colorful past included a stint as a professional wrestler, Swartz had haul-seined his way from Lake Erie through the Chesapeake Bay to Hatteras Island. Swartz decided that haul-seining wasn't the best way to go on Pamlico Sound, so he cut up his seines, reworked them into pound nets, and used his oyster scow to hoist croakers out of the nets. "Bob's only happy when he's working," explained his wife Florence. "Where was I on my sixtieth birthday? Out in the woods in Murfreesboro, cutting down pound-net stakes with Bob and a bow saw." When Swartz turned eighty-eight, a hundred Hatteras Islanders turned out to celebrate. After dinners of fried turkey and grilled rockfish, fishermen crowded around Bob and Florence for a group portrait. One of those fishermen was Paul Dunn.

Paul toiled with Swartz, Dorothy counted pennies, and they finally had enough money to buy their own boat. Swartz knew that Paul had the drive and would strike out on his own. He gave Paul his blessing, and thereafter the Dunns were under a spell that was both an enchantment and a curse. Fish was their life: he caught it, restaurants bought it, and she brought it, tray by steaming tray, to hungry diners. And in recent years as a fisheries activist, she fought for the privilege to continue with this mixed blessing of a lifestyle, serving as president of the Hatteras-Ocracoke Auxiliary of the North Carolina Fisheries Association.

She took the anglers' drink orders and recited the specials of the day. "Bluefish, gray trout, or fried oysters, with two vegetables. Twelve ninety-five."

"Is the bluefish fresh?" one of the windburned anglers asked.

"Why yes sir, it is," Dorothy assured him, as she placed four ice waters on the table. "That fish was splashing in the net just this morning. I'll be right back to take your order."

"Hmph," muttered the man with a shake of his head. "That's where all our fish went! They ought to outlaw those damn nets."

"Is that why you didn't catch nothing, Bo?" hooted one of his companions. Dorothy's face betrayed nothing. She had heard her share of insults toward Paul's livelihood, but still she never failed to feel a twinge of anger. Outer Banks locals have long learned to take the mixed blessing of tourism in stride. Still, the irony of serving seafood to people who blamed commercial netters for their own lack of luck was unnerving. Dorothy fought the temptation to point out the contradiction between her customer's politics and his culinary choices, and tossed her sun-bleached bangs away from her eyes.

"I'll be right back with those drinks, fellas."

In summer the front porches of island restaurants and stores sag under the weight of newspaper boxes carrying the daily news from Richmond, Washington, Baltimore, Norfolk, and Raleigh. Like brightly painted toy-soldiers, the boxes line up in even formation, offering news to Outer Banks visitors not quite willing to "forget it all" during their vacation. With the approach of winter, locals reclaim their communities and dig in for the chilly, windswept months ahead. The newspaper bins disappear with the tourists, and only the boxes cradling the *Virginian-Pilot* ride out winter. Some find it odd that the Norfolk-based *Virginian-Pilot* is the year-round paper for Outer Bankers, instead of the state's own capital-city paper, the *News and Observer*. But a human pipeline from Hatteras Island to Virginia has existed since waterways ruled the paths of trade and commerce.

The Outer Banks totter precariously at the mercy of the Atlantic, serving as the easternmost barrier between North Carolina and the moody blue sea. The only highway, often over-washed and impassable, shows how tenuously the islands are linked to the rest of the world. Folds of sand swirling behind cars on the dune-bordered highway remind motorists that asphalt can, at Mother Nature's bidding, instantly disappear under a coastal desert. Quick reckoning and the instinct to dig in, come hurricane or wicked nor'easter, are traits born into coastal natives.

A streak of independent thinking has always defined the Outer Banks character. Nineteenth-century Hatteras Islanders joined Hyde County, across Pamlico Sound, to form a provisional government in protest of their state's efforts to secede from the Union, and they established Hatteras as the capital of the "true and faithful state of North Carolina." A Hatteras preacher was named governor, and the against-the-grain Bankers made an unsuccessful attempt to send their elected congressman to Washington, D.C. "The actual de facto jurisdiction of this Government is confined to the sand-bar recently captured by the US Navy at Hatteras," wrote a *New York Times* commentator. "The portion of this bar protected by the US flag may be fifteen or twenty miles long, by about one mile wide. Would it not be a hazardous experiment to reconstruct the political edifices on such a foundation?"

The sandy Banker villages, fringed by maritime forests, mountainous dunes, and yaupon bushes, continue to be removed from the influential muscle of Raleigh, Durham, and Chapel Hill. "Live and Let Live" is the unofficial motto of islanders who had naturally assumed that North Carolinians to the west would reciprocate their laissez-faire attitude.

Snippets of anticommercial fishing rhetoric began drifting in from the westward reaches of the state in the 1980s, moving east across broad Pamlico Sound like jumbled, abrasive radio reception. Dorothy Dunn heard it on the lips of tourists, and disturbing words showed up in print, such as "trawling kills," "nets are weapons of mass destruction," and "sport fishermen to arms!"

"Nets and trawls must be removed from North Carolina waters," wrote sports columnist Joel Arrington in the Raleigh *News and Observer*. Describing encounters between commercial and recreational fishermen during a bluefish run off Nags Head, Arrington claimed that watermen lost all sense of civility in their pursuit of profit. Netters, he maintained, swooped in with their boats and nets, "snatching" the fish away from unsuspecting sportsmen. "To end injustices like those on our beaches," he asserted, "fish stocks must be allocated increasingly to anglers."

If villagers dismissed Arrington as a solitary voice, his growing fan base and letters of support proved quick correction. Anglers from inland counties wrote about "greedy netters who have continued for years to rape our shores." Supporters of a ban on commercial nets warned against the "frontier mentality" of watermen, and advised anglers to "remember what the commercial people did to the buffalo, passenger pigeon and ducks."

"Fishermen feel that they, simply by place of birth, have the God given right to rape our coastal waters," wrote an angler. "Unless we want to be historically significant by depleting to extinction our state fish, the red drum, and other species that have blessed our waters for countless years, then we had better get the haul seiners off our beaches, get the menhaden boats out of sight, and get the shrimpers out of the sounds and estuaries."

Arrington encouraged readers to join the state chapter of the Coastal Conservation Association, an organization founded by Texas oil magnates Walter W. Fondren III and Perry R. Bass in the late 1970s. The well-funded angler club, backed by sportfishing boat and tackle companies, angler magazines, and other businesses standing to gain from an increase in recreational fishing, spearheaded "ban the net" and "gamefish" campaigns throughout Texas, Alabama, Mississippi, Louisiana, and Florida. Boasting a powerful membership that grew to include some U.S. Cabinet, Congress, and Senate members, the CCA responded to criticism that they ignore the impact of net bans on fishing towns with the statement, "Fisheries management is not welfare."

Tarheel fishermen were loath to see that the "conservation con" had reached their shores, as it became clear that there was more going on than a heightened environmental awareness. This was shaping up to be a full-blown culture war.

"It is maddening to pick up a statewide newspaper and read such biased and inaccurate articles," said Sandra Kellum of Bettie. "Joel Arrington would in one swoop put thousands of men out of work, devastate entire communities, rob Eastern North Carolina of its oldest industry, and deprive the public of its right to seafood. This is an assault on our jobs, our well being and our way of life."

But the CCA found North Carolina to be a particularly nettlesome target, with powerful coastal legislators not easily swayed that a healthy marine environment rested on the elimination of commercial fishing nets. "North Carolina is a national embarrassment, an albatross around the necks of sportsmen, environmentalists, and fisheries professionals from Maine to Florida," complained columnist Ted Williams in the popular magazine, *Fly Rod and Reel*. "Fishermen are in denial–emphysema patients sucking on cigarettes–long cut off from the rest of the planet."

At the end of the night, Dorothy Dunn hurried through cleaning the dining room, making it ready for the next day's breakfast rush at Tides. Paul would be asleep before she got home. He'd fished for so many years now, he couldn't stay awake much past ten because he was up before dawn each morning, even on blow days. Her thoughts of Paul brought back the irritation she felt from her earlier encounter with the sportsmen. If only her customers knew what it took to get fresh fish on the table.

Above her station hung a painting depicting a tight row of recreational anglers and their four-wheel-drive vehicles with toothy racks of PVC rod holders, parked rib to rib at Cape Point. The artist captured the excitement at the Point when bluefish or red drum are running. Few places in the sand are more coveted than Cape Point, the elbow of the Cape Hatteras National Seashore jutting out into the Atlantic Ocean. Men and women stand in the rolling surf, attached to the sea by thousands of yards of monofilament line, hoping to experience the best fishing Hatteras Island offers.

In contrast to the sportsmen, a dozen crews of no-nonsense seiners patrol the beaches each fall from Corolla to Ocracoke. The crews are made up of fathers, sons, granddads, and nephews. They scan the seas for signs of fish: ripples and splashes in the water, subtle changes in shades of blue or grey, diving gulls and pelicans. After spotting a school, the crew blasts through the surf in a small dory with the net playing out behind them. The daring-do scenario does not play well with anglers watching from the beach with fewer bites than they'd like.

Anglers and netters are both welcomed at Cape Point, at least in the eyes of the law. "Congress created a paradox when they created this park," reflected the superintendent of the Cape Hatteras National Seashore. "They said residents will retain the right to earn a livelihood by fishing. Then they said the Secretary of the Interior may make rules and regulations to protect recreational uses.

"The problem at Cape Point," he continued, "is that the seine-netters are a visual irritation to anglers. What we have here is a social issue."

The superintendant's assertion was supported by statistics showing that the commercial landings of bluefish accounted for only 10 percent of the total landings, and of that amount dory haul-seine crews were responsible for less than 5 percent. "I think many sport fishermen would be surprised to learn that recreational fishing is the major cause in the decline of bluefish," said National Marine Fisheries Service's Dr. Ed Christoffers in *Field and Stream* magazine.

"There's worse fishing every year," disagreed one of the recreational anglers who fired off letters to newspapers, politicians, and fisheries commissioners. "It's because there are too many nets out there. That's why recreational fishermen can't catch fish. I think netters ought to go offshore a couple of miles so all of us can have some fun."

Watermen believed the problem at Cape Point was blown out of proportion by a few vocal anglers, whose war drums reverberated miles inland to those with poison pens. Actual confrontations in the surf were few and infrequent. "While I've heard various complaints ranging from verbal abuse to nets encircling surf fishermen," said Jerry Schill of the North Carolina Fisheries Association, "no names, no vessel numbers, and no license plate numbers have surfaced."

As disgruntled anglers turned up the volume of vehemence in their letters, politicians threatened to take legislative action if the marine fisheries commission didn't "do something." Commercial fishermen decided it was better to take a hit on the chin rather than risk losing it all. A summer of public meetings had taken its toll. Neighbors greeted neighbors at the community center's front door and then took their seats, netters on one side of the room and sport fishermen on the other. There were no chairs for fence-sitters. Unnerved by the passion erupting over Cape Point, one recreational fisherman told his wife, "This has the potential to tear this island right in two." Worn down after weeks of meetings, commercial fishermen offered to not fish within a one-half-mile radius of the tip of the Point, hoping this would appease anglers, who couldn't bear the sight of nets, while still allowing their boats to stay in the lee of the wind.

"If that's the price the industry has to pay for peace, great," said Jerry Schill. "But within the next month somebody will want the commercial fisherman to inhibit his way of life even further, to the point where he can no longer feed his family."

Fishermen had learned a hard lesson about the power of the printed word. They were stunned to comprehend not only the depth of vehemence outsiders felt toward their profession, but how effectively the media flamed the fires. The daughter of one waterman summed up how Outer Banks families regarded the capital city newspaper that regularly published diatribes against them. Until the *News and Observer* started publishing the facts, she wrote, "the people of coastal North Carolina will continue to use it for its true use—a mullet wrapper."

Future fishermen of America.
Photo by B. Garrity-Blake

Sealevel fish house.
Photo by B. Garrity-Blake

Fish House
Opera

"Irene's talking about ordering a new mattress and box spring," said Wayne Basnett. He leaned against a culling table and watched as fish-house manager Michael Peele hosed down the worn wooden floor. "I suspect she's called Manteo Furniture already but she won't admit it," he added with a shrug and a smile. It was early afternoon and Basnett's bluefish, just hauled out of Pamlico Sound, lay iced in boxes stamped with "Fresh Seafood" in large green letters. The fish house sat beside a saltmarsh creek on the sound side of Hatteras village. Net reels, crab pots, pound-net stakes, and the rusted shell of a pickup truck decorated the yard.

The men stood in the cool, cavernous interior of Quality Seafood, poised between the front entryway of trucks and commerce, and the back door opening to quiet creek waters. A daily theater unfolds in small community fish houses, scenes of humor, advice, teasing, disappointments, obligations, expectations, and familiarity. The players are fishermen, dealers, neighbors, and kin, but roles blur and relationships intertwine in a small town. The wooden floors, one moment slick with scales and slime and the next hosed down clean, form the stage. Fish boxes stacked neatly, "poly-dac" rope snaking across the floor, and work gloves dropped here and there serve as props. The gurgle of diesel engines mixed with static from VHF radios plays a background symphony to the subtle dramas that unfold.

"What do you think that'll run?" Basnett asked as he cracked open a Pabst Blue Ribbon. He waited for Peele to respond before taking a swallow. Peele, keeping one ear open for the tell-tale rumble of Quality Seafood's eighteen-wheeler on the narrow road running through the heart of the village, told two young boys to make up more cardboard fish boxes.

"Well," Peele finally replied, "I believe I paid maybe nine hundred for a new bed. But that was a while back, after the tide came up in Hurricane Emily." Basnett grunted and chugged the beer. He stood tall and stretched.

"Sometimes I get out of bed at night and sleep on the floor when my back's bothering me," Basnett complained. His voice was thinly peppered with remnants of the tidewater "high-toider" accent that is fast disappearing since newcomers and television diluted the lilting island dialect. Slowly easing Peele to the point at hand, Basnett jiggled his PBR and downed the rest of it.

"So," the fisherman said, tossing the can into a pail full of Styrofoam coffee cups, empty Coke cans, and Nab wrappers. "What's Old Billy Blue Eyes saying about prices on croaker? Bluefish?" One sidelong glance from Peele told him prices were not good. "Worse than last week? What about trout?" Peele, moving a large stack of crates on a dolly, gave the fishermen a thumbs up on gray trout.

"Okay, buddy," Basnett said after pulling off his cap and running his fingers through his thinning hair. "I guess I'm headed back to Frisco. I still need to find that coupling. You think Nacie might have one?"

"Good chance of it," said Peele, walking Basnett out of the cool fish house into the blaring Carolina sun. "Lord knows, that man never throws anything away." Basnett's pickup sat beside a mound of pound nets that the Peele family would mend, dip, and set for flounder in the fall.

"I know one thing," Basnett muttered while climbing into his truck. "I spent all week catching nothing but a mattress–and I'll be lucky to afford the boxspring."

The tenuous trust between fishermen and dealers suffers when wholesale prices tumble. "That son-of-a-bitch looked me straight in the eye and told me he shouldn't have any problem moving my trout," a fisherman complains to another. "Then I get a nickel less than your guy paid! He had his excuse made up before I walked through the office door." Fishermen regularly accuse dealers of collusion and price-fixing, and on one occasion filed a formal complaint with the state. The complaint got nowhere. Nor have attempts on the part of fishermen to form cooperatives.

Michael Peele was used to fishermen stressing out over prices. "Some fellas get so mad they stop selling here," he remarked. "It happens a lot. In time fishermen come back pretty well, too. But things are getting tight for everybody in the fish business. Look around." He scanned his yard on the creek. "Commercial docks are being torn down to make room for marinas and waterfront houses. Developers look at my fish house and see a pile of splinters and boards and rust on top a gold mine. They figure it's only a matter of time."

Peele's uncle Nacie had deeded him the property. "There's been a fish house here as long as I can remember," he declared, wiping sweat off his shaved head. "As long as I live, there will always be a fish house here." His was not a lone operation, however. Peele's fish house was part of an impressive network that moves a highly perishable product fast and far.

"Quality Seafood in Elizabeth City leases this operation. They have a large facility up there with four or five tractor-trailers that carry fish to Philadelphia, New York, all points north and south, all across North Carolina, to big markets and small ones too. They've got a crab-picking house and a cutting house. Sometimes they get big contracts with Winn Dixie and Food Lion. So there's more to this than people think."

A crabber interrupted, announcing "I'm moving my stand tomorrow. Bad water's moved in." Peele shook his head and knocked his ice

"As long as I live, there will always be a fish house here," Michael Peele. Photo by Susan West

machine into operation. Keeping things cold and clean has always been at the heart of the seafood business. The machine thudded and rattled, spitting out a heap of blue-white ice chips. "Years ago," he yelled, "ice was shipped in, covered in sawdust and buried in the ground. Can you imagine?"

The sound of a diesel truck competed with the noise from the ice machine. "Back in the old days cows and pigs ran free on this island," he added. "Then they started penning them in, reducing their grazing space. Well, the same thing's happening to fishermen." The forty-eight-year-old offered a sad half smile. "The commercial industry is being corralled up." Peele stepped outside as a large tractor-trailer nosed down the dirt road into the fish-house yard.

Gray trout, called weakfish by bureaucrats and Yankees, is a winter gem to Outer Bankers. Tarheel fishermen land more than 70 percent of all commercial catches on the East Coast, and most of those fish move through fish houses in Dare County. Boatloads of fat, sow trout, hauled in by gill-netters braving a winter sea, have caused money to rain all over Hatteras Island. Teenage boys, off-duty waitresses, carpenters with time on their hands, and school teachers looking for an extra buck show up in force to sort fish or shovel ice at fish houses during the winter trout runs.

"A 75 percent cut? No, I don't think so," fishermen told each other when word of a proposed quota reached their disbelieving ears. The reduction, proposed by the Atlantic States Marine Fisheries Commission, threatened not only fishermen and fish dealers but businesses like Burrus' Red and White Supermarket, Ballance's fuel docks, and the village's branch of East Carolina Bank.

The women of Hatteras Island mobilized their forces in the face of potential catch clampdowns. Dorothy Dunn and other fishermen's wives of the Hatteras-Ocracoke Auxiliary approached the Hatteras Ladies' Fire Auxiliary and asked for help. The volunteer fire department had been hosting fish frys for close to fifty years and welcomed the opportunity to join the cause. Fish dealers helped advertise the fry and donated hundreds of pounds of trout.

"No, I always mix the hushpuppy batter," a white-haired woman responded when a fisherman's wife asked whether she could help. Each fire department volunteer guarded his or her area of expertise. The women brewed iced tea, fried hushpuppys, and dished cole slaw and potato salad onto plates. Behind the fire department, in a building specially designed for the purpose, a handful of men worked the fish fryers.

Enough money was raised to foot the bill for Hatteras Island fishermen to attend meetings from Virginia to Rhode Island, starting in Annapolis in 1994. "That Annapolis meeting was a real eye-opener," recounted gill-netter Dave Blackmon, who named his boat *Servant*. "Some of the members of the technical committee made it very plain that our presence in the audience was a hindrance to business as usual. No one was interested in what we had to contribute. I mean, why bother to ask fishermen about mesh sizes?"

Blackmon, called Bub by fellow fishermen, removed his glasses and rubbed his eyes. "The meeting ran for four hours before the committee realized they were using two different tables and the incorrect formula for calculating exploitation. I didn't leave there feeling too comfortable about the people in charge of protecting this resource."

Jeff Oden, another Hatteras fisherman who had traveled to Annapolis, was equally nonplussed. "The scientists had a problem with the drop in gray trout landings from 1989 to 1993, and the fish seemed to be getting smaller. But they didn't want to hear our explanations. The decline in landings was from fewer boats fishing for trout! As any gill-netter can tell you, the warmer the water, the smaller the fish. Between '89 and '92 the winter water was almost like bath water. But no one wanted to hear any of this."

The fishermen insisted that they were seeing more gray trout, and bigger gray trout, contrary to the data offered at meetings. When asked about the discrepancy between the scientists' stock assessment and the fishermen's observations, one scientist responded, "Fishermen see what they want to see."

"I'll tell you what I see," said Jeff Oden. "Fish managers who expect us to believe that they know how many trout are in the ocean. They can do this sitting behind some desk? Without input from the very people who give them their data, the fishermen? It's like counting jellybeans in a jar without looking at it!"

Oden, a compulsive fisherman even by Hatteras Island standards, could walk away from fishing and help his wife run the family motel if he ever got fed up with political assaults on the job he loves. "Jeff's just miserable here at the motel," said his wife Katie. "He moans and groans and the next thing I know he and his father are into a tiff over how to fix a toilet." Contrary to his reputation as a doomsayer, Oden still had enough confidence in his fishing future to contract for a new, larger vessel from a Maine boatbuilder.

The punches thrown at fish houses and gill-netters hit home when the government threatened to close federal waters to gray trout fishing altogether. The North Carolina Fisheries Association, the largest commercial fishing trade organization in the state, filed suit against National Marine Fisheries Service. They were joined in the lawsuit by the state itself, a move that raised the hackles of recreational fishing groups. "On the face of it, a closure in federal waters sounds like a strong conservation measure," explained a state attorney. "But our scientists looked at the multispecies nature of our fisheries and the potential for a shift in effort to state waters. They concluded that the closure would result in a higher discard mortality." The state offered alternatives but, according to the attorney, "NMFS refused to even consider those."

To the astonishment of fishermen accustomed to losing political battles, a federal judge ruled in their favor. "It made no difference what anybody said," opined the United States district court judge. "The decision to close federal waters wasn't based on fact. The scientists were deliberately misleading someone." Watermen could not believe their ears. They felt vindicated–but also a little sick that their worst suspicions about science and management were warranted.

"Using 1980 as a statistical base year, the government builds an impressive argument of the fishery's decline, sounding the alarm that the fishery is in danger of catastrophic collapse," the judge continued. "What the government failed to emphasize, however, was that 1980 was the greatest year in terms of landings since World War II. Had the agency chosen 1964 as the base year, the fishery would be considered in good health today. If you tell people something long enough, they begin to believe it."

A few gill-net boats pulled into Quality to unload their catches. The din of the conveyor belt took on a steady rhythm, dancing with the chug of diesel engines. Fishermen shouted over the noise as an assembly line of glistening fish moved by and boys sorted them into baskets according to size and species. "Listen buddy, I had that exact problem with my hydraulics. Now, let me tell you what I did."

"Anybody hear anything about that wreck up in Kinnakeet last night?"

"I'm thinking I'll hang more three and a quarter. That caught pretty good last year."

"No, I didn't get in them today. Shoulda headed towards the south'ard with the rest of the fleet."

Michael Peele shoo'd two black Labs out the fish-house door and walked back to the culling table. "I've got a son and I threatened to beat his tail more than once if he became a fisherman," he shouted, tossing a large mullet into a metal tub. "He's a massage therapist in Raleigh." As the last fish was slung into a basket, Peele hit a button and stopped the conveyor. He softened his voice in the quiet. "I'm the last one in my family to do this. I have boats. I have nets. I have a fish house. And I have nobody to pass down the ways of fishing to." He wiped his hands on a rag, stepped out into the sun, and crossed his tattooed arms. "Part of me would love for my son to be a fisherman. But fathers worry about everything shutting down."

Unloading shrimp at Luther Smith and Sons, Beaufort.
Photo by B. Garrity-Blake

"You can't chunk a rock without hitting a fish doctor," Monk Gillikin, Beaufort Fisheries net house. Photo by B. Garrity-Blake

Fish
Doctors

Elbert Gaskill rounded the shoal and headed straight from Harkers Island to Cape Lookout, feeling the big red sun on his face as it bobbed up on the horizon. It was a "slick ca'm" spring morning with no wind or wave. His thirty-eight-foot wooden fishing boat, the *Sandy V*, plowed a straight part in the water and set in motion a long, rolling wake.

Gaskill, an unassuming, quiet man embarrassed by his reputation as one of the best watermen in Carteret County, rounded Cape Lookout and made a beeline for the gill net he had set the night before. Even from a distance he could tell that something unusual had happened. Half his corks had disappeared, and the water swirled. "What in the world?" he muttered. He'd caught something, but not a mess of sea mullet, trout, or croakers. He threw the throttle into neutral, then reverse, sidling up to his set.

"Oh me," he told the whale that glanced up at him from inches below the surface. "Just as I thought." She was a small humpback, about thirty feet long, and she was tired. A portion of the gill net was wrapped around her tail. "Hmm. Hung up pretty good, ain't you?" She rolled slowly to the surface and took a spluttering breath, then let the water barely cover her again.

Elbert Gaskill thought a minute. She must have gotten entangled early last night, judging by how tired she was. He had a good sharp knife with him. Should he try to free her himself? He pushed that idea out of his head and picked up the radio. The humpback could put up a struggle and capsize his boat. Besides, Gaskill had an endangered species on his hands, and he knew that he was required to notify the federal government. He only hoped that his troubling catch did not bring about a firestorm of unwelcome publicity.

Gaskill called the Coast Guard and the Coast Guard called National Marine Fisheries Service in Beaufort. While waiting for the NMFS team to arrive, Gaskill and the whale kept an eye on each other. "You'll be on your way in no time," he assured her, hoping his words would come true.

Times had changed since Gaskill's grandfather's era, when dolphin- and whale-processing plants dotted the coast. Damon Gray of Hatteras Island remembered the porpoise-processing operation there, when fishermen would seine the marine mammals, gaff them by the blowhole, and haul them ashore, thirty or forty at a time. If dusk, the crew would leave the porpoises beached and breathing through the night. Gray's job was to stab them in the heart under the left fin. The men skinned the porpoises and carted them to the factory for processing, where the fat was rendered for oil and the skin sold for use as industrial belts.

A bottlenose dolphin had recently washed ashore at Corolla and was treated like an orphaned baby. It was rushed to the NMFS lab in Beaufort, christened "Benny," and adopted as a media darling by the wider public. Over two hundred citizens volunteered to stand in a cold tank to hold Benny upright, tube-feeding him around the clock. "It makes your day to hold a dolphin's heart in your hands," said a volunteer, shortly before a Coast Guard plane airlifted Benny to a more sophisticated laboratory in Florida. Many tears and tax dollars later, Benny died.

Gaskill scanned the waters, wishing the NMFS team would hurry up. The last time a humpback was entangled in a fishing net, just off Pea Island, the Hatteras Island Rescue Squad tended to it. The unconventional rescue attempt proved a physical and intellectual challenge to squad members more accustomed to rescuing lost windsurfers and boaters. Although the whale was successfully freed, federal officials chastized the squad chief for assisting the whale before an authorized marine mammal specialist could arrive.

A wheezing sigh broke Gaskill's train of thought; the whale took another breath and sank a couple of inches below the water "Hang in there, now," he said. "Y'be all right."

Gaskill wasn't far from the original site of Diamond City, the nineteenth-century whaling village on the Shackleford Banks side of Cape Lookout. One hundred years ago, this whale would have been hauled ashore and named—not to humanize the creature, but to etch the event in memory by bestowing the catch with the name of the crew, the spot where it was taken, or its distinctive markings. The whale, considered a blessing, would be cut up and divided among Diamond City families for processing. Elbert's wife Sandy was a descendant of Josephus Willis, captain of the Red Oar whaling crew of Shackleford Banks. The crew, comprised of Willis and his six sons, killed the Mayflower whale, one of the last leviathans harvested in North Carolina. The skeleton of the Mayflower, all that remains of the toughest fighter in the history of

Tarheel whaling, hangs today in the North Carolina State Museum of Natural Sciences in Raleigh.

Harkers Islanders are proud of their Shackleford Banks whaling roots. Forced to abandon the Banks in search of more sheltered land after a series of vicious storms flooded houses, exposed coffins, and drowned livestock, Diamond City families sawed apart their cabins, loaded them on skiffs, and sailed them over to Harkers Island, Marshallberg, or the Promised Land of Morehead City. Those sailing to Harkers Island rebuilt their homes on land bought for one dollar an acre. Today, lots in subdivisions with names like "Whaler's Ridge" and "An Island Way of Life" fetch many thousands of dollars an acre.

Elbert Gaskill had never found a whale in his net before. Snagging a cetacean in a fishing net doesn't happen every day along the Atlantic coast. The industry was taken by surprise when, in 1994, Congress reauthorized the Marine Mammal Protection Act, mandating that fishing gear-related deaths of mammals be reduced to "insignificant levels approaching zero" within five years. Fishermen were skeptical that entanglements were enough of a problem to warrant such a strong directive. "It was like telling someone a UFO is going to fly into your yard and get tangled in your wife's clothesline," said a National Marine Fisheries Service staff member.

Congress called for the formation of regional take-reduction teams, composed of scientists, environmentalists, state bureaucrats, and commercial fishermen. Their task was to come up with a consensus plan on how best to avoid interactions between marine mammals and commercial fishing gear.

Several North Carolina gill-netters volunteered to be on the Mid-Atlantic Take Reduction Team for harbor porpoise, but in the end were disappointed to report lack of consensus. Although the team agreed on a number of ways to reduce entanglements, a bone of contention over the use of "pingers" tarnished the group's sense of common purpose. Pingers are acoustic devices that deter porpoises from approaching nets. Fishermen wanted to recommend that research be undertaken on the use of pingers for the Mid-Atlantic region, an idea supported by NMFS staff.

"Unfortunately," the fishermen wrote to the NMFS director, "a Mid-Atlantic pinger study was adamantly opposed by one member of the team–Dr. Andrew Read of Duke University." Read, assistant professor of marine mammalogy, baffled fishermen with his opposition to the idea of pinger research. In 1994, a New England study showed "that acoustic alarms reduced the incidental catch of harbor porpoises in sink gill nets." The report concluded that "the use of acoustic alarms appears to hold considerable promise" and recommended similar field tests. Andrew Read was one of the principal investigators in the experiment. And in 1996 the Gulf of Maine/Bay of Fundy Harbor Porpoise Take Reduction Team, of which Read was a member, recommended research to determine "the effectiveness of pingers in times and areas where they have not been used."

But in the Mid-Atlantic team, Read argued against spending federal funds on a pinger study, cautioning that additional animals might be taken. The crux of the letter explained that "it has just come to our attention that Dr. Read is a co-investigator on a current research proposal titled, 'Do Acoustic Alarms Reduce Bycatch of Bottlenose Dolphins in North Carolina Gill Nets?'," which was submitted to North Carolina Sea Grant in April 1997.

"Dr. Read's proposal was under review at precisely the same time he thwarted consensus and argued against the usefulness of an industry pinger study. He never indicated to the team that he had a grant under consideration nor did he provide a copy of the proposal to solicit input from industry members on the team." The fishermen stressed that "group consensus was a victim of personal and academic gain."

"It has come to my attention that a group of fishermen from the Mid-Atlantic team has written a letter to you," said team-member Sharon Young of the Humane Society to the NMFS director. Young listed Dr. Read's credentials and called him a "distinguished scientist and an honorable man," unfairly called into question by the "mean-spirited and poorly conceived" objections of fishermen. Young urged the director to "see through the fabricated accusations in the letter from fishery representatives."

Andrew Read, defending his position, wrote that two other marine mammal scientists on the team as well as two conservationists shared his opposition to the fishing industry's pinger study proposal. He argued that there was no conflict of interest because his proposal "would be funded from a completely separate and independent source." Read explained that his proposal "focuses on bottlenose dolphins, not harbor porpoises," and would not involve "using actual nets." Read didn't explain why an industry-led, Mid-Atlantic pinger study was a bad idea, but expressed regret over not disclosing his study to committee members. He stressed that his opposition to the fishermen's proposal was simply because it was an "unnecessary" and "ill-conceived experiment."

Watermen are not blind to concentrations of money, power, and ego lurking within the folds of a burgeoning marine science and management bureaucracy, and they question the image of scientists as purveyors of objectivity who stand above the fray of coastal "user-conflicts." "You can't chunk a rock without hitting a fish doctor in Carteret County," said a net-mender at Beaufort Fisheries menhaden factory, referring to marine science facilities operated by Duke University, the University of North Carolina, North Carolina State University, the National Marine Fisheries Service, and the North Carolina Division of Marine Fisheries, all within a ten-mile radius of his net pile. "Fish doctors" is the local term for biologists, oceanographers, ecologists, and social scientists who are forever measuring, sampling, testing, observing, and recording all things marine-related.

"Here we go," Elbert Gaskill told the whale, as the Marine Mammal Stranding Network from NMFS came zipping through the water at last. Vicky Thayer, head of the team, greeted Gaskill and surveyed the situation. "Maybe we can untangle her without cutting your net," she offered. "Why don't you start taking it up slowly." Gaskill hauled most of the net aboard his boat until the whale, uncomfortable with the change in tension, began to thrash about.

"Slack it off!" called Thayer. Gaskill gladly complied, as the whale threatened to flip his vessel.

"Well, I guess we should go ahead and cut her out," Thayer said, shaking her head. Gaskill sliced through the mesh, and the humpback swam off with a small swath still attached to her tail, as if waving good-bye with a ragged hanky.

Thayer, sensitive to the negative press fishermen receive when it comes to their encounters with endangered species, made sure to comment publicly on Elbert Gaskill's role. "I want to stress how cooperative Mr. Gaskill was," she told reporters. "We all were striving for the same purpose—to free the whale."

Elbert Gaskill, not one to bathe in the limelight, steered clear of the press. But his wife Sandra had something to say. "We want people to know," she emphasized to reporters, "we aren't trying to do harm."

Nets in a Down East yard.
Photo by B. Garrity-Blake

A Penny
Hurts

"It's like the men smother if they don't fish," Sandra Gaskill said in a soft voice, her fingers combing through the fringe of the throw pillow on her sofa. When a wife sees her husband off to sea, a small cloud of worry hangs in the sky, no matter how bright the day. Commercial fishing is the most dangerous occupation in the country, and politically it sits on the fringes with very little government or public support. The *Jobs Rated Almanac* ranks "fisherman" as the worst occupation outside of lumberjack in terms of pay, job security, stress, and potential growth. Fishermen's wives are in a tough place: Their men believe that fishing is in the blood, as natural and essential to them as breathing, yet that work is in dire straits. When a man calls himself a fisherman, he figures that pretty much covers who he is and how he fits within the universe—a threat to his occupation can bring down his whole world.

"A wife has got to be spunky and say 'don't worry' even though you're worried sick," Sandra continued. "I've been in the bedroom so many times and said to myself, 'God, what am I gonna say to him this time?'" She and her husband Elbert were proud of his honest profession, and nothing mystified them more than the hostility commercial fishing garnered from those who lived upstate.

"So many people against you, trying to take you off the water for good!" Sandra dipped her head and looked over the top of her glasses. "When we go on vacation in the mountains we don't go around wondering how we can starve people to death or take their jobs away."

Mrs. Gaskill was especially upset about sport-fishing organizations that poured endless money and energy into trying to cripple her family's livelihood. "It's not our fault sporters can't fish as good as our commercial fishermen can. I think part of it is jealousy. If they're lawyers or something, well, our husbands don't know as much about law as they do."

"I gave my daughters two bits of advice," said Mildred Gilgo. "Go to college and do not—do not—marry a fisherman. They took my advice.

They saw the bad times first-hand." She paused and added, "They saw the good times, too."

"I'll wake up and tell Mike about some romantic dream," reflected Edwina Tosto. "He'll say 'All I can dream about is a damn shrimp boat!' He can't dream about nothing good. When he was laid up with a bad back, he'd hear the trawlers out there at night, and say 'That's a 453' or 'That's a caterpillar engine.' He was a fish out of water."

"People think fishermen are ignorant because they aren't verbal," observed Carolyn Mason of Bettie. "They don't talk much because they don't state the obvious." Her husband P.D. fished from Pamlico Sound to South Carolina. "Have you ever heard the radio jargon? The chatter? It's shorthand, hard for you or me to understand. But that's how they're used to communicating.

"These are intelligent men," Mason stressed. "They'd be dead if they weren't."

Dale Brooks lived on Harkers Island with her husband John, not far from Sandra Gaskill. "John has nothing on paper," she said. "No degree, no certificate. But if you give him an engine, he can take it completely apart and rebuild it without a manual. It's kind of like playing piano by ear instead of reading music. Fishermen work by ear."

Harkers Islanders were famous for "working by ear" rather than by written plans. Boatbuilders constructed impressive wooden vessels by the "rack of the eye," having an uncanny ability to judge weight, displacement, and balance without so much as a written calculation. Using an archaic term from their Shackleford Banks whaling ancestry, Harkers Islanders proudly proclaimed themselves to be "proggers," or beachcombers, with a history of making do with whatever washed ashore—timbers from a wreck, scrap metal, rope. Fishermen were jacks-of-all-trades, surviving with skills in carpentry, mechanics, navigation, and meteorology, plus a healthy dose of common sense.

Islanders say they're "mommicked" or beat to death trying to make it on the cusp of the twenty-first century. The shore along Harkers Island is less accessible to proggers and fishermen, as trees are cleared for waterfront homes with docks representing the imposition of private property rights on land once thought of as communal. Fewer locals can afford to live in their home community—the highway leading to the island is bordered by trailer parks full of young families who attend island churches and send their children to Harkers Island School, but who live "off island" because of sky-rocketing property costs.

Dale Brooks worked as a full-time commercial fisherman with her husband until she figured she'd better prepare for the world that was changing before her eyes. With her heart in fishing but her mind on an uncertain future, she studied computers at the local community college and landed a job at Cherry Point Marine Corps Air Station. "Now I'm bringing in steady money," she sighed. "I get sick leave, insurance. Fishing–you don't go fishing, you don't get paid. I decided I better establish myself apart from fishing. If anything ever happened between me and John, I just couldn't continue to fish and compete with him." She was hired at Cherry Point on the spot. "I explained to them that I was a commercial fisherman and anybody that was a fisherman has got to be a hard worker. They said, 'She's ready, she's willing, she can do it.'"

Brooks had fished with her father since she was a small girl. "I remember going with my father, and coming in and seeing John with his father. His Dad used to comment, 'Yeah, you gotcher little helper with you!'" After high school she boarded John's boat and headed for South Carolina. "All I wanted to do was just get out of school. John said, 'Come on with us.' I said, 'Yeah, shoot. I'll go down there with you.' Me and John would go nights instead of his dad, who was getting old. After standing on the boat all day he could go home and rest that night. We'd get groceries and head out."

She fished with her husband for ten years. "We'd rake clams, or go shrimping with either a double rig trawl or a little boat with a single net. In the wintertime we'd go scooping or dragging for scallops. We have 1,500 yards of net, and we'd go sink-netting offshore. I've gone fly-netting with John and his Dad on their fifty-footer, the *Del and John*, that they built. I went shrimping with them off South Carolina for two or three years. I've been sea scalloping with Bentley and them on the *Captain Kenny*." Brooks pointed to a large collection of seashells. "That's how I caught all these conchs."

Brooks knew several women who fished with their husbands. "John's Aunt JoAnn shrimps with Benjamin. She'll help him steer and cull, and Benjamin will pull the doors and wind back. It is physically hard for a woman." She took a deep breath and shook her head. "Picking up hundred-pound bags, dumping them, hauling clams in the truck. A woman's got to be tougher'n a lighter knot, as they say around here. See, the trees grow these roots in the ground and people'd use them in the old days for starting fires because they're so solid of a wood. They call 'em a lighter knot because you can start fires, they'll burn forever.

"You've got to be tougher'n a lighter knot because fishing is the hardest living in the world," she reflected. "You never know what's going to happen. Your boat might sink. Hurricane come by and wash the shrimp out. Cut yourself or have a heart attack. And there's no health insurance because it's so expensive for someone self-employed. It can all flip right out from under you so quick."

The fish house is the watermen's gateway to world markets. It's also where the freedom of open waters bashes into economics. "A fisherman's not totally independent," Brooks pointed out. "He's got to depend on that dealer. Otherwise he'd need his own deep freezer, walk-in cooler, ice-maker, large fuel tank, fish truck that can run to New York—well, you get all that from the fish dealers." She sighed. "It's a love-hate relationship, sometimes. Dealers say 'You stay in my harbor and I won't charge you rent but you got to sell to me.'"

Brooks leaned in and said, "I think the dealers are in cahoots. And it's just plain hard to work your butt off all day and come in and have to just about give your stuff away. The dealers say to each other, 'You pay nine cent a clam and I'll pay nine cent.' The price is sixteen cent a clam right now, so a thousand clams is a hundred and sixty dollars. If the price ain't but twelve cent a clam, it's a hundred and twenty dollars. So *every penny* counts. A penny hurts."

Brooks admitted that her new job made life easier financially, but it changed her relationship with her husband. "He gets in those spells where he feels guilty that I'm still having to work that steady pace when he's slacking off for no fish or bad weather. He'll go to Cab's, the local store up here, and they'll tease him—say, 'You got it made, she's at Cherry Point making money while you sit here and drink Cokes and eat cakes.' He laughs but I know it gets to him. It doesn't bother me if I'm working a little bit more than him in the winter. I try not to measure anything like that."

"But don't think I don't miss the water. I still go fishing every chance I get." Brooks's eyes sparkled. "There is nothing I love better than those summer days when we get up bright and early with the sunrise. Jump in the car, get a biscuit, and drive to Cedar Island. Get on the boat and it's pretty all over the sound." She swept her hand out before her. "That smooth ride, you set in the boat and it's just as cool. I took a Friday off the other week just so I could go clamming. Sometimes we go clear to Ocracoke, a good twenty-two-mile run. You get such a sense of freedom running across Core Sound or Pamlico Sound to the clam beds. If there's no stinging nettles or man-o-wars or boom jellies to burn you up, it's a good day."

Twins "Leadline" (Deidre) and "Corkline" (Bridget) love to go fishing with their father, Gordy Daniels. Photo by B. Garrity-Blake

"These shores and shoals are a retreat to many a troubled mind and a peace to the soul,"
Mildred Gilgo, heading shrimp with Lennie Saunders.
Photo by B. Garrity-Blake

Wave of
The Future

"The stinging nettles are bad toward Portsmouth Island this time of year," noted Patrick Hill. "So last week we worked in Old Drum Inlet." Hill was a commercial fisherman like his father, and the two often fished as a team. Core Sound's Old Drum Inlet, directly across from the village of Atlantic, had filled with sand until the inlet no longer provided a passage to the ocean. But its shoals were productive, and the bottom was an easy reach for clammers.

"We thought we would catch around four or five hundred clams if we put in a long day because Old Drum Inlet gets worked right much," Hill said. "But I had seven hundred on June ninth, and every clam was a littleneck. The next day I caught one thousand. The banks is a funny place, catch some one day, the next nothing."

Core Banks was visible from Hill's hometown of Stacy, near Atlantic, Sea Level, and Cedar Island. The sandy barrier island is made up of wind-shaped dunes, sea oats, ground cherries, glasswort, wild asparagus, and wax myrtle bushes. The banks appear to hover in the east across the calm waters of Core Sound, a thin, shimmering line of sand dividing the blues of water and sky. The fragile-looking ribbon of sand has held back the mighty Atlantic for almost 18,000 years, since rising sea levels broke through the dunes and flooded the lowlands, creating Albemarle, Pamlico, Bogue, and Core Sounds.

Core Sound, with meandering shoals and migrating grassbeds, is a safe haven for fishermen with boats too small for the open waters of the Atlantic. It is one of the most heavily worked bodies of water in North Carolina, seasonally raked, dredged, trawled, and netted. Designated "outstanding resource waters" by the state, Core Sound remains the healthiest and cleanest body of water around. Fishing families who have lived off its shrimp, fish, crabs, and clams for generations are downright reverent about the area.

"I'm twenty-six years old and never had another job except working on the water," Hill wrote to the Division of Marine Fisheries, concerned that a portion of his favorite fishing grounds was about to be turned into private property. Seven people had applied for ten-acre leases just off the western side of Core Banks for shellfish farming operations. The new seventy-acre conglomerate would be a cordoned-off area of water totaling more than three million square feet, or sixty contiguous football fields, all attached to an existing seven-acre lease farmed by the person who set the precedence—Joe Huber. A wiry man well aware of his controversial reputation, Huber earned the nickname "Joe Hard Crab" after moving from Florida to North Carolina to make a living potting crabs. It didn't take long for the prospect of aquaculture to capture his imagination, and his nickname changed to "Joe Slick" after he built a hatchery and moved his family into a new three-story, plantation-style waterfront home that loomed over his shoreside leases in the village of Atlantic.

Rumors began circulating that Huber's wealth came not from clam sales, but from state grant money obtained through his partnership with University of North Carolina scientist Charles "Pete" Peterson. "The state is supporting a program that is supported by grants," said one of Huber's neighbors. "You take away the grants and see how long these clam farms stay in business!" As far as Huber was concerned, the acrimony toward his business was purely a matter of ignorance and jealousy.

"Nobody cared a doggone thing about what we were doing until they saw we were making money at it," he said, dismissing naysayers as too narrow-minded to catch the wave of the future rolling their way. Huber presented himself to legislators and scientists as a born-again fisherman who had forsaken the traditional, "destructive" techniques of wild harvesting in favor of aquaculture, the only fishery that "gave back more to Mother Nature than it took out." When he sought to expand his operation to include acreage off Core Banks, his neighbors failed to see how Joe Huber's enterprise was giving back more than it took. This was the last straw for those who feared that private claims to public-trust waters would infringe upon the average person's ability to scratch out a living on the water. Not only did Huber want what many considered to be too much for one man, he was the first to lay claim to the easternmost frontier cherished by generations of Down Easterners.

"Core Banks is sacred to us," explained Mildred Gilgo of Atlantic. "These Outer Banks and shores and shoals are like a retreat to many a troubled mind and a peace to the soul." Many Down Easterners were descendants of the "Ca'e Bankers," nineteenth-century Core and Shackleford Banks whaling villagers. Until the federal government designated the Banks as part of Cape Lookout National Seashore, families had cabins on the island. Going to the Cape on weekends was a time-honored excursion. Men prepared steaming pots of clambakes, women strolled the beach, and children learned how to "sign" clams, spotting keyhole shapes in the sand.

Although begrudging the loss of their cabins when the National Park Service took over the island–several folks burned theirs to the ground to rob the government of the satisfaction of destroying the shanties themselves–Core Sounders staunchly believe in the principle of common property for their beloved banks.

"Yesterday in church–it was Easter–the preacher told a story that I hadn't heard since I was a little girl," said Mrs. Gilgo. "Jesus didn't have any money to pay the tax in Capernaum. But he turned to Peter and said, 'Cast your line and the first fish you catch will have a gold coin in his mouth.' When Peter came back he had the money to pay his tax. That's how we've lived–from hand to mouth–and the Lord has always provided for us." She paused. "Core Banks is our heritage. It belongs to me and it belongs to you. It's a strip of Outer Banks where only God Almighty has the authority to say who can walk on it, who can fish on it, and who can clam on it. If you grant these leases, may God have mercy on your soul."

When state legislators hear the words "commercial fishing," their eyes glaze at the thought of this political no-winner: small communities full of strong-willed people with incomes on the modest side, pride on the high side, and, as Governor Hunt remarked, "heart-tugging" stories to tell. When they hear aquaculture, however, some perk up with futuristic, world's-fair visions of fisher-scientists in white lab coats using the latest in environmentally friendly technology to feed the world.

"On a sparkling, sun-dappled morning last week, Mac and Amy Willis reached into the shallow waters of Newport River and pulled up a bagful of the future," read an article on aquaculture, touting it as the evolutionary "next step" after commercial fishing. Shellfish farming represented "freedom from the past, a stride into a new way of life, one where man exerts more control than ever over the vagaries of commercial fishing. The Willis' are no longer hunter-gatherers. They are truly farmers of the sea."

Growing clams and oysters on privately held leases was not new in North Carolina. Many traditional fishermen acquired small leases of their own to take part in state-controlled "relay" programs, moving shellfish out of polluted waters to clean-water leases. But these "gardens" were not in the same league as intensive, private-culture operations, the largest of which entail land-based hatcheries, nurseries, and in-water cages and mats. A few growers hold not only bottom leases, but water-column leases as well, giving them exclusive rights to the water from the bottom to the surface, barring public boating, fishing, or swimming within the designated area.

"If Jesus came back to earth today," declared Lennie Saunders of Atlantic, "he'd not be able to walk the waters of Core Sound."

"Give me clean water, flood and flow, then I'll give you oysters," declared grower Jim Swartzenberg at a forum on water quality and shellfish. The success of his farmed oysters depended on the crop being suspended high in the water column on racks, away from bottom sediments. Although quick to tout his business as progressive, and proud to acknowledge the state's assistance in his efforts, Swartzenberg made the point that aquaculture was not quite the darling of state government that traditional fishermen thought. "It's a numbers game," he stressed. "We have to make twenty-five bushels to the acre. We plant oysters in the spring and wait two years in the fall to harvest—a two-and-a-half-year turnover. So I've got to make fifty or sixty bushels an acre to make production. Who wants to take up a business where the government is holding an ax over your head?"

The criteria in granting shellfish leases are simple. State employees sample the area, and if their samples equate to ten or more bushels of clams per acre, the lease is denied and the area is declared a "natural shellfish bed." If fewer than ten bushels of clams are sampled, however, the area is declared nonproductive and the lease may be granted. "There are a lot of places, such as Grass Lump Creek, that are sandy bottom and the clams are not catchable due to cold water, northerly winds, and so on," said Patrick Hill, questioning samples taken during cold weather. "My father and myself have tried many a place in winter and late spring and caught *nothing*, only to go back a month or two later and do good. This is common knowledge to fishermen." Sampling of Joe Huber's proposed lease on Core Banks yielded 1.4 bushels of clams per acre, to the astonishment of his Down East neighbors, and the area was approved as unproductive bottom of little use to the public.

"But one bushel of clams will equal 250 chowder clams, 400 cherrystone clams, or 600 littleneck clams," an Atlantic resident calculated. "At ten cents each, 1.4 bushels of cherrystone clams would earn a clammer fifty-six dollars. I think I would be correct in saying that many clammers would consider fifty-six dollars a decent day's work."

"A natural shellfish bed is ten bushels an acre," responded the secretary of the Department of Environment, Health, and Natural Resources in Raleigh, "not a decent day's work as you describe."

Coastal forests are logged for pulpwood and timber, fields are paved for new shopping centers and restaurants, and unimaginable amounts of storm water rush into estuaries and bays. "Fecal coliform bacteria are found within the guts of humans and other warm-blooded animals," explained Dr. Mike Mallin of the University of North Carolina at Wilmington. "Impervious surfaces prevent natural water filtration—the water can't percolate down through the soil, and comes bouncing up and rushing downstream, carrying with it whatever has been deposited on those surfaces. It leads to delivery of untreated runoff water to shellfish beds and human contact waters."

After heavy rains, shellfish beds are declared off-limits to commercial harvest until tests show safe levels of biotoxins. About 54,000 acres are closed temporarily each year in North Carolina; 364,000 acres of coastal waters remain permanently closed. Parasites like Dermo and MSX, which ravaged native oysters, also take their toll. In 1994 Governor Jim Hunt created a task force called the Blue Ribbon Council on Oysters to examine the problems.

The council presented recommendations on restoring the depleted oyster fishery. Although methods of dealing with declining water quality were outlined, pollution took a back seat to the first recommendation in the report: beefing up aquaculture. The council advised the state to encourage private aquaculture operations with new lease procedures, new oyster culture research facilities, and state-funded studies.

"When the oysters clean the water, the people who are around the water, including those who have beaches and sailboats, are a lot happier," observed a Duke scientist on the council. He pointed out that oysters and clams are filter feeders and help clean impurities out of the water. "All those leased oysters produce larvae, they're going out to the public bottom," he continued, suggesting that a beneficial side effect of shellfish farming was the seeding of surrounding public areas.

"I feel a lease would not help us as one of those biologists said it would," Patrick Hill countered. "He said that the clams on the lease would spawn and drift to other areas." Hill pointed out that clam farmers, unlike public harvesters who could only take clams that were one inch or larger, could harvest clams at any size, and usually chose the small ones, which had not reached full sexual maturity, but which were most profitable. "People who have leases harvest the littlenecks, not a spawner, to make their money."

"The Blue Ribbon Oyster Council sealed our fate," maintained Mildred Gilgo. "It all started with the $350,000 in tax money spent for them to come up with those recommendations." She acquired the minutes from every council meeting, filling two large three-ring binders. Her tireless efforts at collecting and scrutinizing state studies and documents led her husband Charles to call her "the detective."

"It's here in black and white." Mrs. Gilgo's copy of the minutes was marked with her yellow highlighter pen and notes. She pointed to a quote from a scientist pondering how they can "sell" the idea of privatizing public resources, and to another where a committee member suggested printing brochures for "commercial fishermen and so forth–the ones who can read."

Four days before the public hearing on the proposed Core Banks leases, fisheries officials made good on a challenge presented by several fishermen. "Let us sample those Core Banks sites that you think are unproductive. *We'll* find the daggone clams!"

State biologists had accompanied the group of six to the proposed sites. The resulting "supplemental report" stated that the fishermen rejected the division's method of taking random samples from plastic bottom frames. "Citing unfamiliarity with the use of the sampling frames and a firmly held belief that clams could not be raked from bare, sandy bottom at this time of year, the fishermen chose instead to use a modified, stratified random sampling pattern." In short, fishermen dug in grassy areas where they expected to find clams.

The Division's previous sampling had turned up a total of two clams in 480 samples. The fishermen, who worked for three hours, raked 198 clams in 139 samples. The supplemental report attributed the fishermen's success to "the highly targeted and clumped nature of the samples." It concluded that these new figures represented a little over two and a half bushels of clams an acre, still well below the ten bushels required to deny leases. It conceded, however, that "this supplemental sampling does point out the need to further assess the suitability of leasing the sea grass areas contained in the proposed lease sites."

"Hundreds rose up in the protest of it," recalled Pam Morris in reference to the Core Banks hearing on the day after Easter. "We were devoutly against it." People packed the courthouse that April evening, and the crowd seemed to hold its collective breath with every testimony. "Look around and see how much territory has already been taken away from the fisherman," declared a fisherman, standing at the podium before state bureaucrats. "Core Banks is prime clamming bottom. Why in the world do you want to take it away from the public and give it to just two or three people?"

A handful of clam farmers, bravely participating in a gathering not too far removed from the old pitchfork-and-torch scenario, were likewise angry at state officials for letting a bad situation get worse.

"Don't give grants, don't give money, don't promote shellfish leasing, unless you're going to give people a way to do it," said applicant Jerry Wolfe. "I don't need to be investing my time and money in something unless I have the okay of the people that are around it. We either do it right or we don't do it. And we get a comprehensive plan and we think it through. And we work it out." He looked out among the sea of tense faces in the courthouse. "And we do what's really right for everybody."

The conciliatory note struck by Wolfe vanished with Joe Huber's feisty testimony at the end of the evening.

"Everything I got I worked for," Huber said, challenging the room with angry eyes. "I started on the water as a commercial fisherman. I set crab pots and I worked day and night just like all of this crowd." He faced the officials and leaned into the microphone. "And I saw us killing the resource. In another ten years there won't *be* a commercial fisherman in North Carolina."

The courtroom silence broke into guffaws and angry remarks as Huber continued. "Fishermen say that aquaculture doesn't generate any money for the community. Well, they don't know nothing about economics." He turned and faced his hecklers. "Every dime spent to the grocery store or paying taxes or whatever, comes back in one form or another." Huber then hurled fighting words. "You can laugh about it because you probably don't pay no taxes. I pay my taxes." A state biologist tried to restore order as the clam farmer, in small-town, Harper Valley PTA-fashion, began singling people out by name, accusing them of hypocrisy, lying, and vandalism. After the hearing, a procession of cars and trucks carrying fishermen left Beaufort and headed east, red taillights glowing.

Before the Division of Marine Fisheries decided whether to approve the new applications, legislators stepped in and temporarily banned new leases in Core Sound. "It's a shame people had to go to their legislators instead of the division to get this done," said menhaden factory owner Jule Wheatley. "I was with the Marine Fisheries Commission for eight years. We heard the same outcry two years ago and told the division not to accept any more applications of Core Banks. It wasn't done."

"These fishermen," reflected Joe Huber, "better understand that they are a minority. The sooner they understand that, the sooner they'll understand what's going on."

Patrick Hill understood what was going on. "I know I'm never going to get rich. And I don't want to. All I want is the opportunity to go to Core Banks where I can get in a good day's work. All fishermen need is a place to work."

View from Avon Seafood, Hatteras Island, North Carolina.
Photo by B. Garrity-Blake

Ol'
Drum

"She liked to have killed me," laughed Leon Scarborough, welcoming an opportunity to share one of the multitudes of stories that makes up Outer Banks history, a history measured locally by memorable catches or by poor seasons. "Irene and I had just bought a brand new '72 Blazer. Mind you now, this was our family car, not my beach rig. Flounder had never been any thicker than on the beach that winter! I believe it was Bobby Scarborough who rigged up a net behind his truck. He had a door on the outside end, a staff on the inside, and he drug that net down the beach catching loads of fish."

"So, Monford Austin says to me, 'Come on, Leon, let's take that Blazer of yours and give it a try,' and we did. We pulled the back seat out and stacked it with sixteen boxes of flounder. Flounder were running up front under the accelerator. This was our family car! Irene wasn't too happy with me," said the sixty-five-year-old, beaming with the mischievous grin that's protected him throughout his marriage, making it hard for Irene to harbor much of a grudge.

Scarborough settled deeper into his recliner in the den of his small and immaculate home in the heart of Hatteras village. His house sat on the edge of a narrow, barely paved road leading to Quality Seafood in a part of the village where the smell of fish still translated into the smell of money.

"Oh, I've been fishing off and on most of my life, but I remember the exact minute I knew I'd fish for good," said Scarborough. "I was still in the Coast Guard and I set a net back of the station. Well, when I checked it, I had four puppy drum. That's what gave me the fishing bug and sealed my future–four puppy drum," he laughed. "When I got out of the Coast Guard, I bought some net from the preacher, fifty crab pots, a battery for flounder gigging and a battery charger, and I was ready to go."

Irene, a Block Island native who had traded the rock-strewn coast of Rhode Island for the bare beaches of Cape Hatteras and the teasing grin of Leon, stuck her head in the doorway to the den. "Leon, are you *still* talking fish?"

In the brewing battle between those who fish for fun and those who fish for a living, no scaled creature inspired more emotion in North Carolina than red drum. Maybe it was because drum has a lifespan that rivals that of people. Maybe it was the heft, strength, and sheen of the fish wrestled out of the water. Or perhaps it was how the drum emitted a deep, rhythmic croak, as if offering its captors a wish. Red drum was more than another saltwater catch. It was a swimming, feeding, and spawning symbol to sportsmen and watermen alike.

The angler group calling itself the Coastal Conservation Association handed out bumper stickers in the shape of a red drum that say, "Join CCA!" When the CCA was begun in Texas, the group's first victory was getting red drum designated as "gamefish," off-limits to commercial fishermen. "It's time for North Carolina to follow the lead of other states in making the sale of red drum illegal," wrote sports columnist Joel Arrington. "The official state saltwater fish is far too valuable as a draw for anglers to fritter away in the marketplace."

The commercial value of red drum in North Carolina has never been high, although it was harvested in sufficient quantities to support canneries like Croatan Drum in Wanchese before World War II. Today's market is local, as Outer Bankers have long enjoyed a traditional dish called Ol' Drum. Ol' Drum is a name reserved for the granddaddies, the monster fish that do not give up their saltwater lairs without a struggle. These man-sized fish were stewed and seasoned with pork drippings and onion and served with potatoes.

"Native Outer Bankers salted the drum before they had refrigeration. Now they freeze it," explained Murray Fulcher of South Point Seafood in Ocracoke. "Big red drum are as much a part of the heritage of Outer Banks and Down East Carteret County natives as buffalo are to the Indians and whales are to the Eskimos." When Beach Buggy Association bumper stickers commanding people to "PROTECT RED DRUM" made their way to the Outer Banks, more than one local doctored the sticker, resulting in the taillight commandment to "EAT RED DRUM."

When fishermen caught wind of strict new regulations proposed for the red drum fishery, they smelled something rotten. Sports columnists were touting the red drum issue as a battle cry. Recreational fishermen were "marching to the beat of red drum," wrote Joel Arrington, excited at the prospect of a CCA victory in the intractable Tarheel state. Fishermen were especially suspicious of the proposed rules, however, because the timing seemed off. Officials spoke of an impending stock collapse at the same time large schools and big fish were sighted both in the ocean and in the sounds. Even the sports columnists saw no contradiction between calling for gamefish status of the "threatened fish" and gleefully reporting that the "big bronze battlers are everywhere!"

"Where do you fish for red drum?" John Ochs asked state biologists meeting with fishermen in Buxton. "I can't recall ever seeing any of you out there on the water. I've seen Rudy Gray, I've seen Johnny Willis, I've seen my friends, commercial and recreational fishermen, but I've never seen any of you."

A passionate hunter for what he called "the prime rib of the sea," Ochs helped supply his family's Frisco restaurant with fresh fish. The Quarterdeck Restaurant was nearly as plain inside as outside. A few autographed photos of major league ball players hung on the wall, and a large fish tank provided the only diversion other than watching waitresses race out of the kitchen door, careening through the dining room with heavy trays of oyster and trout combos, Hatteras-style clam chowder, or the sacred stewed drum. Ochs kept the tank filled with fish, shrimp, and urchins, which he'd donate to the state aquarium each November after the restaurant closed for the winter months. Not long after Ochs spoke up at the meeting and criticized the biologists' sampling techniques, two marine patrol officers walked into the Quarterdeck and charged Ochs with possession of two undersized drum that were swimming in his fish tank.

The proposed red drum rules were disturbing enough to fishermen, including new trip limits, a requirement to attend gill nets, and a prohibition on keeping the "Ol' Drum"–fish larger than twenty-seven inches. But what inspired Outer Bankers to make the arduous four-hour drive to a Marine Fisheries Commission meeting in New Bern was a sense of outrage that citizen participation in management was getting reduced, not expanded. The newly formed Northeast Regional Advisory Committee, which included the Outer Banks area, had requested the commission to postpone their vote on red drum rules until the advisors could meet and discuss the recommendations.

"I'm very displeased," said a co-chair of the Northeast Committee, "that our request to postpone this meeting was denied. I think this Fisheries Reform Act is going to work, but we need to have the proper process and timelines."

But no one was prepared to witness the reception Bill Foster received from two of the commissioners. Foster was not only a knowledgeable fisherman with a strong background in biology; he was a former member of the very commission he stood before. The dozen or so others from Ocracoke and Hatteras who came to testify were glad Foster was among their ranks, because he didn't simply describe his season-to-season observations–information scientists had a habit of dismissing as "anecdotal." Foster came to meetings armed with data, charts, and the same vocabulary as fisheries biologists.

"There has been no attempt to estimate stock size," Foster told commissioners after a detailed critique of Marine Fisheries Commission data. "If there is no estimate of stock size, then what evidence is there that the stock is declining? There has been no attempt to quantify either the losses to the adult stock or the recruitment to the spawning stock. The fact that there are very old fish in the population contradicts the escapement rates and F values estimated in the 1996 assessment.

"The most obvious recommendation," he concluded, "is that someone needs to analyze the tagging data."

"Thank you, Bill," said Chairman Jimmy Johnson, preparing to call the next speaker. But Commissioner Kurt Fickling interrupted him.

"Your education is a marine biologist, is that right?" Fickling asked Foster.

"That's right," answered Foster. "I was doing the research for my Ph.D. dissertation."

Fickling folded his hands. "Do you have a Ph.D.?"

"No," responded Foster, "I did not finish writing that letter. I went fishing instead."

"You have a master's degree?" probed Fickling.

"Yes," Foster affirmed. "I've completed all the Ph.D. course work, did the research, had it three-fourths written, but didn't finish."

Folks attending the meeting, as well as some commissioners, shifted uncomfortably and traded glances. It was highly unusual for a member of the fisheries commission to engage in a dialogue with a member of the public during hearings.

"So you got an undergraduate in marine biology," continued Fickling.

"Master's degree in ecology," corrected Foster.

"And then you were working on your Ph.D. and was that in marine biology or what?"

Bill Foster moved his large frame from one leg to the other. "Fisheries biology. My dissertation topic was the management implications of the life history of the red drum."

"Some of the data that you cited here," inquired Fickling, "you did it in your own research?"

"Figure two in the handout, that's my data. I was the first one to age the drum using otoliths. At that time, there were a lot of people who didn't think drum lived to be fifty years old. But yes, I did collect that data."

"Thank you, Bill," said Fickling.

Chairman Johnson, relieved that the exchange was over, began calling the next person up to the podium. But at that moment commissioner Pete Moffitt pulled his microphone close to his mouth and boomed, "Through your research do you find any difference between the life history of red drum in North Carolina as opposed to South Carolina, Georgia, Florida, Mississippi, Louisiana, or even Texas?" Moffitt, like Fickling, held a seat on the commission reserved for an experienced sport fisherman.

Foster returned to the microphone. "I am honestly not qualified to speak for other states," he replied. "I don't have experience in them."

"I'm wondering," Moffitt continued, "why you would think we have an escapement rate above 30 percent when I talked to Dr. Charlie Wenner, and he thinks the escapement rate may be 17 percent."

"If I had to guess...," began Foster.

"Let's don't guess now," said Moffit with a small smile. "We're talking specifics if you're holding us to specifics. All of the state representatives and lead scientists tell me that red drum in their states is severely overfished. Why would I take your hopefully unbiased opinion and give it greater credence than I would those I've worked with?"

"I hope," said Foster, "that you would take my comments and ask for review of them. I'm proposing that there's no need to rush to judgement, there's time to assess this thing and see if we can come up with a better estimate of what the mortality of escapement is."

Moffitt shook his head. "I agree that your word should be spread around, but it should have been done before today. All of a sudden somebody comes up and gives me a paper that's unpublished, that has no peer review to it, and it's what you personally claim. I've known you for a long time and I hope we've been good friends, but I just can't accept this."

Chairman Johnson could stand no more. "Let me break in here. If commissioners want to ask questions of the speakers, fine. But let's not enter into a debate."

"Mr. Chairman," responded Moffitt, "my point was that I got a lot of people that I get input from and why should I accept a paper that I disagree with?"

"Bill," interjected Commissioner Fickling, "you did your undergraduate work in the seventies, right?"

Foster exhaled deeply. "Undergraduate in the sixties."

"Well," said Fickling, "like Pete, I'm trying to figure out what your background is in red drum, and how you draw your conclusions, because I have a problem with some of those conclusions."

Stunned by the tone of Moffit's and Fickling's questions, Foster later remarked, "As far as I knew that was the appropriate time for me to comment. If there wasn't adequate time to consider my information, that's because the commission was in too much of a hurry to approve the rules."

After Foster stepped down, a painful tone defined the rest of the afternoon. Mike Langowski stepped before the microphone and qualified his testimony by saying, "I got a high school diploma and I went fishing instead of college."

"I have no degrees, nothing," testified Joe Wilson, unable to hide the disgust in his voice. "But I'm in the top 3 percent of my class, because according to North Carolina Marine Fisheries 3 percent of us are catching 50 percent of the red drum!"

"I'm seventy-eight years old," declared Ephraim O'Neal from Hatteras. "I've fished ever since I was fourteen or fifteen. I don't have any degrees to qualify as a biologist, but I've studied fish all my life."

The Marine Fisheries Commission voted for the new regulations that evening, despite the concerns of member Willy Phillips. "After listening this afternoon," Phillips cautioned, "I don't think the community believes they had an opportunity to be part of the process. It's worth a second chance to open up a different forum, to where an interplay between anecdotal and biological and scientific can have a legitimate discussion. The opportunity to build respect within the commercial community cannot be overestimated. Further isolation from this process does nothing but reinforce the attitude that management operates independently of their concerns."

In the wake of negative press reports about the treatment of a member of the public, Commissioner Tim Nifong suggested that his group extend an apology to Bill Foster. Three of the commissioners rejected Nifong's suggestion. Pete Moffitt did, however, write a letter that appeared in several coastal newspapers. "For those that feel it was improper to question Mr. Foster's scientific paper," he offered, "I apologize." But to those who appreciated scientific integrity, the letter expressed, "No apology is necessary."

"Fishermen were scoffed at," said Ocracoker Eugene Ballance in reference to his experience on the state and regional red drum fisheries management plan advisory committees. Committee members produced a plan that was passed and implemented in 2001, but not all members were content with the recommendations. Ballance, one of the handful of commercial fishermen who had specifically targeted red drum, objected to designating the fishery "by-catch" only and to the prohibition on catching the giants. "We brought up the importance of large drum time and again as a traditional meal for the people of the Outer Banks. We were scoffed at and told to eat our tradition."

"I don't believe red drum are in as bad a shape as they say," mused Leon Scarborough as he put the finishing touches on a surfcasting rod he was building. "They don't have to make a rule telling us where we can set our nets. Why in the world would I set where I'd catch a fish I can't sell?"

Scarborough had strong opinions on just about everything, and he was excited to find a new way to express them. "Irene and I never thought we'd own a computer. Now I won't even admit how much time I spend on the Internet," said Scarborough. "I started checking out the recreational websites my son told me about. At first I was just 'working the corner.' Then one night people were making all sorts of crazy accusations about commercial fishing on the FishMoJo site and most didn't know what they were talking about. I was getting real hot and pretty soon I figured out how to type a post real quick," Scarborough continued.

"Of course, I had to have a name. There was Bad Fish, Skip Jack, Dune Creature, Mackerel Snapper. What in the world could I use? Then it came to me. Reading those fellows' posts, they all seemed much younger than me, so I called myself Oldtimer.

"Now Mo, the fellow in charge of the site, deleted my very first post and boy did I get hot. I stewed all night long and then sat down the next morning and posted another message. I called Mo a self-proclaimed Hitler, said I was a Hatterasman–something he'd never be–and then gave my real name.

"Irene didn't know what I was up to, and when I showed her what I had written she turned to me and asked, 'Leon, where is Christ in this?'"

"Then I realized I'd said some bad things and I apologized. Since then I've been to Mo's house for a visit and a few weeks ago he fished my nets with me. We caught some nice blues and some trout. The only fish wasted were the two Mo dropped overboard," said Scarborough, unable to restrain the broad grin that spread across his face.

Scarborough turned serious for a minute and said, "Some say commercial fishing will be over within ten years; some say they're going to run us out of the sound; but I'm more optimistic. I think it'll always be here. Tell me, what did the first two Disciples of Christ do? That's right, they were fishermen."

Shaddin' in January.
Photo by B. Garrity-Blake

Pogie
Boat

Jule Wheatly didn't know whether to ready his boats for the next fishing season or shut the whole operation down and put his business out of its misery. It was mid-January 1986, and he had just been through a torturous set of public hearings where sportsmen accused his captains of everything from raping nature to scaring children on the beach. He leaned on the front office desk and put his face in his hands. "Do you see these gray hairs?" he asked. "I'm thirty-five years old! They weren't here when I started out in this business."

Wheatly ran Beaufort Fisheries, the last menhaden fishmeal and oil company in North Carolina. The business had been in his family since the early 1900s. Wheatly's father was a well-known attorney in Beaufort who sent Jule and his brothers to college at the Citadel. But Jule was the only one who maintained an active role in the fish factory, located on the end of Taylor's Creek on the same road where his father's antebellum-style mansion sat. Beaufort Fisheries looked like the Hollywood setting for Cannery Row—weathered wharfs, a giant wooden net reel, rusted metal buildings with rickety staircases, and vessels sorely in need of fresh paint. Wheatley's office was in a trailer-like building near the entryway of the chain-link and barbed-wire fence.

"If anybody calls for me," Wheatly sighed to his secretary, "tell 'em I've moved to Tahiti. They'll find me on the beach drinking rum out of a coconut."

Bobby "Bob-O" Martin walked in the door and removed his cap. "I don't know, Jule," he said. "I know we're washing out the nets and packing it in for the winter, but I'm getting a feeling...."

"Season's over, buddy."

"Maybe so." A smile broke across his face. "But them shads are calling." Atlantic menhaden, or *Brevoortia tyrannus*, is an oily, bony fish kin to herring. The dense schools are caught in huge volumes and processed into a high-protein feed for chicken, pigs, and cattle. The fish are called "shad," "fatback," "bunker," or "pogie," by industry workers, quick to defend the status of their non-seafood catch. "Menhaden is not a 'trash' fish," Wheatly liked to point out at hearings when the worth of his business was called into question. "You eat menhaden every time you go to Kentucky Fried Chicken. When you eat a farm-raised trout. When you take Omega3 oil capsules for your heart. You're using our product when you paint your house. We're the biggest, most important fishery in America—don't call us trash."

On the wall of Jule Wheatly's office was a framed newspaper article about Bobby Martin and his jackpot seasons at Beaufort Fisheries.

"Tell them *shads* to call back in May," Wheatly told him. "I'll be damned if I'll waste the money and fuel to send your crowd on a wild goose chase in January!" After the lucrative fall fishery, when menhaden schools migrated south from Nova Scotia to Florida, *Brevoortia tyrannus* usually disappeared from North Carolina waters until their spring migration north. Wheatly put his face back in his hands. "Oh, my shoulder. Threw it out playing basketball."

"You can't never tell," said Bobby Martin. "Fish might show." At twenty-six, Martin had caught more menhaden in the past few seasons than any captain on the Eastern Seaboard. He was Jule Wheatly's star, his ace in the hole. "William's been flying and spotted some just yesterday."

"After these new restrictions we got on us? Get it through your head, Bob-O. We may never fish again!"

"Aw, c'mon. Ain't so bad!" Martin replied, well accustomed to Wheatly's pessimism. He looked out the window at the afternoon sun dancing on Taylor's Creek. "You gotta think positive."

"Partner, we are getting into some kind of *trouble* all the time," Wheatly insisted. "Just running a business has become a crime. 'You're factory stinks!' 'You spilled fish on the beach.' 'We don't like the looks of your boats.' My God, the sport fishermen *alone* are killing us. You were at the hearings! You heard 'em. I'd like to say something to that S O B who claimed you tried to wrap his boat in your net and sink him! As if we got nothing better to do than chase those little pissants around with 183-foot pogie boat."

"Sport fishermen don't do us no harm," said Martin. "They think they're hurting us, but that's just their own ignorance."

"Look, now," Jule interjected. "I was driving to a meeting in Raleigh last summer, going through farming country. I get behind a tractor going about two miles an hour. Mad? I'm cussing! First chance I get I tear around him. Then I got to thinking—there he is, in the hot sun, sweating, doing his work. And here I am, from out of town, raising hell. Same

thing happens here. People come down and raise hell at the fishermen."
Wheatly unscrewed the cap and took a swig from a bottle of Mylanta.

"I got a hunch," Martin continued. "I can call the men tonight, have
'em ready to go."

"When have we *ever* caught fish in January?" Wheatly asked the
captain. "Huh?" He received no response from the captain. "That's
what I thought."

Before leaving the factory yard, Bobby Martin stuck his head in the
net house where a few old-timers passed the hours mending great and
small rifts. Huge voluptuous piles of nets made up the perimeter of the
shed, mountains of nets that a person could climb up on or crawl into
for a quick nap. Spider webs of net were hung in the center for repair.
Old Levi Beveridge, a thin man with a caved-in mouth and funny white
hat, was captain of the net house, fastest knitter of any.

"Well hello, Bob-O," said Levi. "Don't recall seeing you in church
last Sunday."

"You didn't see me? I must have been hiding in the back."

"I'll be looking over my shoulder this Sunday."

Benjamin Franklin Willis, "B-Flat" to most, was resting in a nest he
had made near the bottom of a net pile. His face was misshapen from a
huge wad of tobacco in his cheek. "S'time, Levi?" B-Flat asked.

"Not quite quitting time yet, Flat," said Beveridge.

"Hnnnnn?"

"Said not time yet!" B-Flat hissed like a snapping turtle.

"Y'better spit before you drown, Captain Flat," grinned Bobby
Martin. Flat slurred, "*Christ!*" Martin sat beside him and told him that
he could catch the biggest jag of fish tomorrow if only Jule would give
him a chance.

"Tear another net, more like it," Levi responded. The men discussed
past torn nets, ripped by shipwrecked Spanish galleons, sharks, artificial
reefs. They reminisced about pulling up old World War II mines, dead
bodies, and automobiles.

Levi announced that it was quitting time. "I'll see you crowd back
here tomorrow if I live another day."

"Feeding these daggone cats is what keeps you coming back,"
remarked a mender, shooing a tabby that had been sleeping on his flannel jacket. Levi Beveridge brought bags and cans of food for the factory
strays, week after week, year after year.

"Nobody else'll do it," says Levi. "When I'm dead and gone these
cats will starve."

"I'd like to know how a cat goes hungry at a fish factory," smiled

Bobby Martin.

At 4:00 the next morning eighteen bleary-eyed crewmen, some black and some white, began boarding the *Gregory Poole*. The Piper Cub pilot had spied the roiling, dark shadows of a large school of menhaden off Cape Lookout the day before, and Bobby Martin called his boss that evening to get the go-ahead. "Prove me wrong, partner," Wheatly warned the captain. "Prove me wrong." Bobby Martin had proven Jule Wheatly wrong on several occasions–proved him wrong enough to pull the business temporarily out of debt and spark a faint glimmer of hope in his boss's heart.

The crew, carrying clothes, books, and magazines, made a beeline to the brightly lit galley, where Robert "Shag" Willis, the cook, was sweating over an industrial-size stove fixing breakfast.

"You come trampling in here making a mess!" Shag hollered. "Get your coffee and move on." He checked the progress of several pans of biscuits, mumbling to himself. "Soon as I can get that Social Security I'm hanging up this frying pan forever. Boys drive me mad as a hornet!"

"He a good cook but he a grump!" said one crewman to another. The crew could say anything in front of Shag because he was nearly deaf.

"That's the truth," said the other. "Last trip? Cook didn't give us no milk 'cept for one day. Get up in the middle of the night for a snack, he's there watching you! Try to get some milk–he's watching."

"Yahz!" responded the other. "Says nobody helps him. Says onliest one working on the boat is him!" The men laughed, received a scowl from Shag, and left with their coffee.

Another crewman entered the galley carrying a small suitcase and a Bible. "Shag!" he yelled. "We gonna catch us some fish today? We ain't had a paycheck in three weeks!"

"You'll get something to eat when I say it's ready, Preacher!" the cook growled.

Up on the bridge, the vessel pilot Marvin Lewis checked his instruments. The captain adjusted the CB and VHF radio settings. The only evidence that the vessel was underway in the quiet darkness was lights from the shore slipping by–the pogie boat was smooth and silent on Taylor's Creek, like a spacecraft gliding past the stars and the moon.

The *Gregory Poole* eased past Beaufort, soft and asleep, and crept by dozens of sailboats anchored dangerously close to the channel. The pilothouse was pitch dark save for green digital lights and a comet-tail glow from the swishing radar. Captain and pilot were riding high, with a spectacular view of Carrot Island and the moon on the water. They spoke in hushed voices, through the steam of coffee. "Pretty, idn't?"

commented Martin. "Right before sunrise. Stars. Quiet." A vessel full of alert men, their adrenaline kicked up by enthusiasm tossed with caffeine, the boat could have been on a secret mission to Mars while the rest of the town snuggled under quilts and coverlets. The captain, navigating the vessel with one finger on a joystick, said that he had awakened every hour on the hour all night long, checking his clock. "I get so nervous. Excited. You just don't know what the day will bring."

"It's a free world out here," observed Lewis.

"Too bad it ain't free on shore," the captain said softly, turning the *Poole* into Beaufort Inlet toward the Atlantic. "I think some of us got bills to pay."

The pilot switched on the main light to find a chart, and they were blinded by their own reflections in the windows. He switched off the light, revealing a wide-open black sea, a bright star on the horizon reflecting off calm waters. One of the crew delivered breakfast to them. The eastern sky gradually turned purple, then pink, until the sun bobbed up and split the difference between water and sky.

With the sunrise came radio chatter like morning birds: "Come on *Del Ann.*" "Come back." "Tell me if you see any shad." "Sure will, *Gregory Poole.*" "Come on *Gregory Poole.*" "Come back, this is the *Poole.*" "Call me if you see any croaker." "Okey Dokey." "Ayeee gotchee pardner."

The pilot, leaning over the chart to prevent it from rolling up, pointed out a route through Lookout Shoal. "Remember when we could just cut across here? Before it shoaled up?" The captain grunted—his attention was on the horizon and on a radio conversation between two trawler skippers.

"Come back, you say croaker?" "No, just shad—looks like machine-gun fire hitting the water." "Sure it's only shad?" "Whooeee!" "Is it junk?" "No, it's nothing but shad."

"Come in, *Frieda Marie,*" Bobby Martin broke in, pressing the radio to his mouth while looking east across the water. "How big're them thar shaaaad? You see any color?"

"Awww, no Bob-O it's shad but it's small. Peanuts."

Peanuts, mammy shad, hairy backs, and squigglers describe classes, sizes, and behaviors of menhaden. The captain and pilot looked at each other and turned the vessel toward the sighting. "Them trawlers think a three-inch fish is a peanut," Lewis observed. Before long the buzz of the spotter pilot was heard overhead, and the aviator alerted the captain that he'd sighted the school. Martin called his mate to ready the crew—he blew a whistle and suited up in yellow oilskins.

The men boarded two forty-foot aluminum purse boats on the stern of the *Gregory Poole* and were lowered into the ocean. The captain was on one boat, and the mate was on the other. Lashed together with a common net, the twin boats sped off toward the fish, visible only by a few splashes and "whips" and a flock of diving seagulls and pelicans. The purse boats separated, playing the 1,200-foot net out between them,

A fair set of pogies.
Photo by B. Garrity-Blake

and the crew encircled the fish like cowboys with a wall of mesh 90 feet deep. When the two boats met again, a crewman dropped the tom weight overboard, drawing the bottom of the net together like a purse and capturing a portion of the massive school. As the men hauled in the slack, the pilot navigated the *Gregory Poole* closer to the wide circle of corks. Things got noisy—the hydraulic powerblock, a net-lifting device, helped pull the seine into the purse boats. The crew heaved forward, digging their fingers into the mesh, and pulled back with their whole bodies again and again. The work was easier than the pre-hydraulic era when crewmen sang soulful work songs to haul all of the net and raise the fish, but it was still tough nonetheless.

The *Gregory Poole* sidled up and lowered a black hose into the heavy set of fish, pumping the menhaden into her hold. Cables screeched, engines roared, and fishermen shouted. Once the net was empty, the crew took off in the tandem boats to make another set.

They set again and again, grabbing the net and heaving back for hours. Fish were pumped on board so fast that a stream of blurred silver poured into the hold. The cables threatened to snap and gears screamed. One fish hold was filled and then another. The sun hopped from the eastern sky to the western. The crew put boards up around the fish holds to extend them by four feet. Fish poured over the boards onto the deck. Someone blew a whistle, and the crew finally stopped, pulling up the purse boats and heading for the galley while pilot and captain turned the vessel toward home.

"Shag! I'm hooongry!" they called, and the cook told them to shut up and get a plate; he had the flu bug and was in no mood.

"You come in here starving and belly achin' and don't shake off the scales till you're inside!" The crew was stoked from loading the boat–fat paychecks were in the near future. They dug in to pepper steak with gravy, mashed rutabagas with fatback, collards, light rolls, and pie. They joked with each other about how they'd spend their money and how excited their women would be.

Up in the pilothouse, the captain eased the fully loaded vessel toward Beaufort Inlet. The sun was almost gone, turning the shore a smoky blue.

"This is the prettiest time on the Atlantic," Martin observed.

"Yep," said the pilot, "and here it is, just for us."

A trawler captain called on the radio: "didya catch a scale thar today Bob-O?"

"Reckon we did okay," answered Martin. "Appreciate your help this morning."

"Okeee dokeeee!"

The vessel eased into Taylor's Creek, sunk low with fish and bumping along the bottom. The captain blew the joyous whoo-whoo-whooo whistle as they passed downtown Beaufort. People along the waterfront honked and waved at the boat. Martin cranked the country music station over the loudspeaker, treating the town to Randy Travis's "Forever and Ever Amen."

The vessel made a final bump, pitching everyone forward, and stood still. The *Gregory Poole* had run aground. But, like the spirits of the crew, the tide was only rising and the captain and pilot would simply wait an hour or so until the vessel floated free. The crew lowered the purse boats and boarded the small craft to finish the journey down the creek to the factory. "This ain't nothing," said a crewman as the aluminum boats pulled away from the *Poole*. "Once we rode like this clear from New Jersey!"

The factory crew would just be starting their shift: bailers preparing to stand hip-deep in fish, vacuuming out the hold of the *Gregory Poole* with a pump, washing the fish into the center of the hold with fire hoses. The rickety conveyor belt would haul fish to the counting machine on the second story. The counter, tallying up the approximate number of fish by the bucketful so the men could be paid accordingly, would turn on a wheel and and dump load after load into the raw boxes, where factory workers crouched and blasted the fish to the next stage with water. The unusual January catch would be cooked, pressed, dried, and ground in this factory that had operated since the turn of the century. "Been many a shad eyeball cooked on this land," said a worker. "I ain't kidding you."

By midnight the entire factory would pulsate with activity, thick columns of white steam oozing from the stacks, steamy bright light spilling out of every window and crack. The interior of a fish factory was as inside as one could ever hope to be, both hell-like and womb-like, flames from the furnace setting off a dark labyrinth of pipes, ducts, machines dripping with cobwebs, and conveyors heavy with fish scales. Rhythmic clanking and churning drowned out any conversation. Zeke, a factory worker for forty years, hosed down the floor night after night near the boilers, fire reflecting off his dark, sweaty brow. Oil vats yielded streams of liquid, thick and yellow as butterscotch. Cats hunched over steaming fish that dropped in small piles from the conveyor above. The smell of toasted fish clung to everyone's hair, clothes, shoes, and skin. "Hot enough for you?" a worker yelled to another. "Devil-man gonna get me anyway—might as well get used to hot."

But the captain was cool and calm on the bridge of the *Gregory Poole*, smoking a cigarette and waiting for the incoming tide. The lights of Beaufort were lovely, and laughter from the docks drifted over the water. "We going out again tomorrow?" Marvin Lewis asked.

"Reckon so," said the captain. "See what the boss man says."

Lewis laughed. "Wha'ya think he'll say? Loaded so heavy our belly's draggin' the bottom!"

"Speak of the devil."

Jule Wheatly called from his car radio. "Been in a damn meeting all afternoon in Raleigh. And I hear the boilers aren't working right at the factory. How'd you do?"

Bobby Martin cut his eyes over to the pilot and smiled. "Fair."

Fish factory cat.
Photo by B. Garrity-Blake

"The family throws it off the boat, and that wreath is free to float around," said Sonny Williamson as Marsha Saunders cast the wreath from the trawler *William H. Smith*.
Photo by B. Garrity-Blake

Blessings

Reverend Bob Carpenter made the hour-long journey from Cedar Island to the shipping port in Morehead City to deliver the Blessing of the Fleet's message. It was a clear October morning painted in Carolina blue and puffy clouds. The Blessing of the Fleet had started years earlier as part of the North Carolina Seafood Festival. But few fishermen participated in the event, despite the fact that the festival was touted as a celebration of the seafood industry. Fishermen, struggling with an unfriendly political environment, saw the festival as little more than a cotton candy and Tilt-A-Whirl attempt to shake money from the pockets of "dit dots," a local term for tourists. And not only was the Blessing of the Fleet held in a remote location too shallow for most vessels, it was held on Friday, a bad-luck day in the eyes of many fishermen.

Everything changed when three Down East women took matters into their own hands. Janice Smith, Sandra Gaskill, and Pam Morris of the Carteret County Fishermen's Association convinced festival organizers to hold the Blessing of the Fleet on Sunday morning instead of Friday. They also insisted that the location be moved to Morehead City's deepwater port, more accessible for vessels and closer to the hub of festival activities. Smith, Gaskill, and Morris doggedly persuaded fishermen to sail in the event. The Blessing soon became the main event of the festival, and one of the few occasions when fishing families and tourists joined together.

"That first year, George Bush attacked Iraq the very day of the Blessing," recalled Sandra Gaskill. "And there we were at the port, where they do all the military deployment. I said, 'Blessed Redeemer, we got in and out of here before the bombs dropped!'"

"I have a friend to Atlantic who refused to come for the first couple of years because it was the Lord's Day and she didn't want to miss church," recalled Janice Smith. "I told her, 'The Blessing *is* church! One Sunday a year set aside special to pray for our fishermen.' Well, she went last year and now she says 'Janice, I'll not miss another!'"

"We have such strong families Down East," remarked Sonny Williamson, one of the Fish House Liars covering the Blessing for a local radio station. The Fish House Liars were Carteret County storytellers famous for spinning yarns and reviving local legends. "The fathers and sons and mothers and daughters all work together in this industry. A lot of these boats have family crews. And the women work in the fish houses, getting the seafood ready for the market. Some pack the fish, drive the trucks, and work the boats."

"The woman is the strong one that can reel that captain in and set his schedule and take care of the young'uns," agreed sidekick Rodney Kemp. "And when the woman says it, the captain jumps!"

From the biggest boats–the *Coastal Mariner* and *Gregory Poole* menhaden vessels–to the smallest of skiffs, dozens of boats fringed in bright blue banners and flags lined up in the water and prepared to pass along the port seawall where a solemn crowd sat in bleachers. The steel trawler *William H. Smith* led the procession of boats, skippered by Marshall "Skeeter" Saunders and crewed by his brother Andy and nephew Doc. "Having a crew of family can be good and bad," remarked Beth Saunders, the captain's wife, who was riding on her husband's boat for the ceremony. "If the boat ever went down, God forbid, look what we would lose. *Everybody.*"

"I thought it was all over, the last time I went out with them," added Lennie Saunders, Beth's sister-in-law. Lennie was one of a tight group of women who had an impact that no fisherman could ever hope to have at meetings–sportsmen and politicians *dreaded* seeing them coming down the hall. These women had no qualms about looking a dissembler in the eye and saying, "Cut the crap."

"I was in the bunk and the bow of that boat was going straight up in the air and then crashed down, over and over. I just knew she was going to come up and flip over backwards!" Her husband Andy chuckled, assuring her that the vessel could easily swamp side to side, but wouldn't likely flip straight back. "Oh, that makes me feel a lot better," Lennie quipped. She grabbed her grandchild, who was trying to run across the metal deck of the boat, and swung him up in her arms. The *William H. Smith* was nearing the port.

"I want to be a model," shouted middle-school-student Marsha Saunders, Lennie's niece. She struck dramatic poses on the bow of the *William H. Smith* and sang Christina Aguilera songs. Her father, Captain Skeeter, hollered that she better be prepared to toss the wreath when he gave the signal.

The 1998 Blessing was especially heart-rending because it had been a tragic year. Not only had the crew of the *Josephine* drowned in February, Captain Jesse Dempsey, Roy Pickle, and John Williams were lost while fishing for grouper off Morehead City on the *Char-Lee II*. A sudden spring storm blew in, and the last anyone heard from them was when the captain radioed another boat that their anchor was stuck and they were going to ride out the storm.

It was just after Christmas when the small trawler *Miss Hillary* went down. After hearing "Mayday! Mayday off the bar," the Coast Guard searched for cousins Manley and Buddy Gaskill from Harkers Island, who'd been sink-netting for trout, sea mullet, and croaker. Coast Guard officers called the search off that evening due to heavy fog, a decision that earned the wrath of Carteret County fishermen and the Gaskill family. The cousins' bodies were found two days later, miles apart. The men had been wearing life jackets, but died of hypothermia. David Gaskill's widow was expecting their first child that spring.

Only weeks before the Blessing, a rogue wave capsized a mullet boat off Core Banks on a beautiful autumn day, drowning Janice Smith's husband Billy and their granddaughter's husband Kevin Daniels. William E. "Billy" Smith, owner of Luther Smith and Son Seafood of Atlantic and Beaufort, was a political heavyweight for the seafood industry. He and his son William Ellis had faithfully attended fisheries management meetings. William Ellis was electrocuted at a fish house in Wanchese, an accident that robbed the seafood industry of a beloved and articulate spokesman.

Reverend Bob Carpenter stood before the podium and regarded the Blessing congregation. Down East families in their church finery, state dignitaries and legislators in suits, and festival goers in shorts and flip-flops looked back at him. If visitors to the Blessing thought Mother Nature, with her storms and rough seas, posed the greatest threat to watermen, they were in for a surprise. Reverend Carpenter delivered a very different and very unnerving message.

"Careful, America, history repeats itself," Carpenter told the crowd. "As we saw with the Native Americans, it is so easy to destroy a people. First you covet their land. Commercial fishermen are losing their waters to sport fishermen. They are getting run off their land by developers who want to fill it with condos, make a fortune, and run. Second, you got to look at a group of people as less than human. Third, the government comes in to control and confine a people to small places. Commercial fishermen are on the receiving end of great social and legal injustices.

"You tell your young'uns, 'See that trawler?'" Carpenter swept his arm out, pointing at the vessels circling in the distance, waiting for the procession to start. The closest boat happened to be the smallest skiff, the bright red *Firecracker*, owned and operated by teenaged fisherman Zack Davis. "Say, 'Look good at him! He may not be here next year.'"

Carpenter gazed out over his congregation. "Who is responsible for this human tragedy?" Some shifted uncomfortably in their seats. "Sport fishing clubs. Real estate developers. Tourists. Politicians. *Everyone* who covets the land, water, and resources." He gripped the podium and took a few deep breaths. "You are living in a time where you can watch the destruction of a people!"

Carpenter's sermon was an eye-opener for folks unfamiliar with the world of commercial fishing. Most had never considered that fishermen were sending up a collective distress flare–not because of the dangers at sea but because of the perilous world of people–the politics, propaganda, and crippling restrictions that were part and parcel of the economic prosperity and growth of coastal towns. Some found it downright shocking that Reverend Carpenter named society as the most formidable threat to watermen, including a visitor who later wrote in the county newspaper that the pastor's social activism was inappropriate for a Sunday morning blessing.

"Sure it was political," responded Carpenter. "I did not take preaching that sermon lightly. I slept very little that week. But I feel I am looking into the faces of the last commercial fishermen, and it tears me up."

After Carpenter's delivery, the procession of boats approached. Sonny Williamson explained to his radio listeners that someone from each boat tossed a wreath into the sea to honor fishermen who had died.

"The fishing vessel *William H. Smith*," announced Jerry Schill. President of the North Carolina Fisheries Association, Schill had migrated from a family farm in Pennsylvania to coastal Carolina, where his appeal to traditional values overrode the odd match of his staunch Catholicism and fierce Republican loyalty with the preponderance of Democrats in the South's Protestant Bible Belt. "In memory of William E. Smith, William Ellis Smith Jr., Julian Saunders, Edgar Fulcher, Norman Robinson, Gary Salter, and Elmer 'Clam King' Willis."

"Okay, girl!" called Captain Skeeter Saunders. Flanked by smaller children, Marsha Saunders positioned herself on the starboard side of the *William H. Smith* as the vessel approached the shoreside gathering. She grabbed a cable with her left hand and gracefully tossed the wreath into the choppy water. All the kids watched the floating memorial as it bobbed along the vessel's wake toward the open inlet.

"A lot of people that are lost at sea are never found," announced Sonny Williamson, pondering the symbolism of the wreath. "The family throws it off the boat, and that wreath is free to float around. Maybe there's some connection there."

Miss Gina of Marshallberg, Core Sound trawler.
Photo by B. Garrity-Blake

"It's a miracle we're still working. A *divine* miracle," Milton Styron working on a net.
Photo by B. Garrity-Blake

Night
Trawl

After their last night together, seventy-year-old fisherman Milton Styron and young federal fisheries observer Chris Jenson ate a hot breakfast cooked by Milton's wife Ruby. The Styrons lived in a modest flat-roofed house on Croaker Street in Davis. Their son lived across the road, and both families cared for several ancient pecan trees and a large garden. The old-timer buttered a biscuit and winked at Ruby in appreciation. He liked to tell about the time, many years ago, when he and his bride took a small shrimp boat from Core Sound clear to McClellansville, South Carolina, with only a chart from the local bookstore and a flashlight to guide them.

"We passed through one place near the North Carolina-South Carolina line in the dark, shining our flashlight from marker to marker. On the return trip home a few weeks later, it was daylight when we passed through there. We saw all the old stobs from abandoned wharfs and fish factories that could have punctured our boat and sunk us if we had strayed just a hair! We were young and foolish." When asked if they had been on their honeymoon, he answered, "Well, yes. And we're *still* on our honeymoon!"

Milton Styron, whose life as a fisherman was mapped on his weather-beaten hands, had worked at just about every type of fishing there was. When the shrimp were running, his small trawler joined several others off Davis Shore, setting off at sunset while tourists nursed their sunburns and bathed their children before bed. As the moon rose, the shrimpers towed in circles throughout the night, the small lights of their boats sliding off the black wake behind them.

The veteran fisherman could remember when no one cared for shrimp, and there was not a great market for the "bugs" that clogged fishing nets and rotted along collard and potato rows as fertilizer. "And crabs too!" Styron explained. "People didn't eat 'em because they were scavengers, bottom feeders. But gradually tastes changed." By the 1950s the market for shrimp picked up, and fishermen began tailoring their gear and fishing habits accordingly.

Shrimp abundance depends on water temperature and salinity, and the crustacean is known as an "annual crop" because shrimp only live one year–what's not caught will die anyway. The larval shrimp float in from the ocean to the shallowest parts of the estuaries and grow rapidly. Bigger shrimp venture out of the bays into deeper waters, where Core and Pamlico Sound trawlers work. At certain points shrimp make a rush for the sea. To get them while the getting's good, fishermen have a science of moon, tide, wind, and the particular habits of the three kinds of shrimp. But dragging an otter trawl is hard, slow, and fuel-guzzling work–a small "try" net is pulled first in order to test the waters for "bugs."

The pink or "spotted" shrimp (*Penaeus duorarum*) show up first each spring if their over-wintering in the estuaries was successful and they didn't freeze to death. "They don't leave for the ocean during cold months and come back like the other shrimp," said Styron. "You see a sign of the spotted shrimp–you can watch 'em grow and move out of the bays into the sound."

Then comes the brown or "summer" shrimp (*P. aztecus*). Summer shrimp are the bread and butter for fishermen who haul them in by the tailbag full all summer long, until the crustaceans make their autumn run for the ocean to spawn. "The best of the summer shrimp is around the full moon in July," Styron said. "Shrimp will run on a moon, from Cedar Island to Harkers Island in three, four days. You catch them on a flood tide. You see them swimming on the bottom with your light, and they turn just as red under the moon. Sou'west wind is best, because a nor'easter will flush them out into the ocean and on they go heading south."

Unlike the mud-burrowing and grass-dwelling species, the white or "greentail" shrimp (*P. setiferus*) are found high in the water column, and fishermen have developed nets that skim the water's surface instead of bumping along the bottom like the otter trawls. Wives and kids love to go greentailing because the water explodes with thousands of popping shrimp that break the surface with their glowing eyes and translucent silver and emerald tails. "Now you catch greentails on a falling tide," Styron emphasized to Chris Jenson as they finished up their breakfast. "But I learn something new and make changes in how I fish every season."

Milton had witnessed a lot of changes during his lifetime, many beyond his control. He found it hard to forgive state policymakers for a series of actions that he found harmful to the livelihood of fishermen.

"It's a miracle we're still working," Styron declared to his young companion. "A *divine* miracle."

Styron, a patriarch of Down East, was known to offer fisheries managers an impressive history of weather patterns, water temperatures, and fish behaviors. "The scarcity of trout you show on your chart," he'd explain, "occurred after the storm of …" or "Do you remember the hard freeze December 22, in 19 and 89? That's why there was nary shrimp in the spring." "On an ebb tide with a nor'east wind …" He could also offer state officials a history of their *own* agency, recalling who the earliest fisheries commissioners and division directors were, when a rule was passed and why.

Styron's deceased twin brother had been a preacher, and they shared a deep reverence for God's creations, particularly the sea and the sounds. He believed fisheries management was a futile and arrogant pursuit, as no person could claim control over Mother Nature and second-guess the Lord Almighty. "When the fish show back up, the biologists take credit. I know different," he declared in an aged but deliberate voice. "We walk with God upon the rising tide, another day of work without the first regret," he wrote in a poem published in the North Carolina Seafood Blessing of the Fleet program.

"Core Sound is worked hard. We haul and trawl across it. We dredge clams and scallops. We set nets and pots and pounds. Core Sound is the most productive body of water around," Styron repeated at public meetings, explaining a theory that struck policymakers as being as counterintuitive as water running uphill. "Not *despite* the fact we work it. But *because* we work it!" Few subjects inspired more emotion in Milton Styron than the productivity of Core Sound. "You say you've got to protect the environment from us, and you restrict us more and more. I'm here to tell you that fishermen are keeping the bottom healthy! Every bay you've closed to us has filled with lifeless sludge."

Milton finished his coffee and looked at the young federal observer across the table. "Chris, you're a good fella. I want you to understand that scientists and bureaucrats are deaf, dumb, and blind to what we're saying." Chris Jenson was sent by National Marine Fisheries Service to study the effectiveness of turtle excluder devices since the TED rule went into effect. He had accompanied Captain Milton for several summer nights on the fisherman's thirty-foot wooden trawler, the *Roy and Mary*. Jenson dutifully recorded the contents of each haul, weighed the amount of fish against the amount of shrimp, noted the presence of sea grass, and counted any turtles that did not manage to escape through the TED.

"Last year," Styron said, "there were eight dead turtles in Core

Sound. The government assumes that commercial fishermen killed every one of those turtles! We didn't kill those turtles. They die of natural causes, they choke on plastic bags. But I tell you, the climate's changed and is getting warmer. We're getting more turtles in our sounds, so the government can expect to find more turtles alive and dead. This all comes down to our livelihood. It should be studied with care, and with the facts!"

Captain Milton pushed back from the table. "Will you do something for me?" he asked Jenson. "Will you write down the things we've been talking about?"

Jenson, who seemed to genuinely enjoy his nights trawling off Davis Shore with the old-timer, agreed to integrate Styron's thoughts in his report.

"The following are my observations working on a Harkers Island-built thirty foot shrimp trawler the F/V *Roy and Mary* owned and operated by Mr. Milton Styron of Davis," Jenson wrote. "Mr. Styron is pulling tandem-rigged trawl nets, both equipped with the Florida fish excluder. Each net has several slits in the wing area to allow fish to escape." "Finfish excluder devices"–or "bycatch reduction devices"–were required in addition to the turtle excluder devices. Years before the equipment became mandatory, fishermen had cut escape holes in their shrimp nets to release as many fish and "jelly balls" as possible.

Milton Styron objected to sports organizations that called discarded finfish "waste," and that petitioned for further restrictions on shrimp trawling to minimize bycatch. "Fish that are caught and discarded are vigorously eaten by laughing gulls and a few terns and brown pelicans," Jenson wrote, reflecting the old man's contention that nothing was wasted on a shrimp boat. "Fish that sink are probably consumed by crabs, other invertebrates, and fish. Overall, very few rotting fish are caught in the net despite towing in the same area night after night."

Jenson made sure to include Styron's struggles with the turtle excluder technology. "I observed two loggerhead sea turtles captured in the starboard net with the Anthony Weedless TED. Both turtles were in good health and vigor, and were released unharmed. This same net had a tendency to either roll or bind up as some of the catch was located in front of the TED. Removal of the catch through the TED proved to be time consuming."

He recounted Styron's opinion that fisheries managers failed to grasp a comprehensive understanding of commercial fishing and did not provide solid rationale for many of their regulations. "An observer should be with a boat or in an area for several seasons. A few observations cannot demonstrate the big picture for any area." Styron questioned the need for excluders in Core Sound, but would not have a problem complying "if there was a sound reason to do so."

Chris Jenson's unconventional narrative, no doubt buried deep in a file somewhere in the National Marine Fisheries Service building in Silver Spring, Maryland, reflected a rare understanding between a waterman and a federal employee.

Milton Styron shook Chris Jenson's hand as the two said goodbye. Jenson repeated that he had enjoyed the nights on Core Sound especially shrimping under a full moon. "But you see the most," said Milton, perhaps also explaining why fishermen see a big picture in the smallest regulation, "during the darkest hours."

Milton Styron setting a net off Davis Shore.
Photo by B. Garrity-Blake

"Let's put her in the meat and go!" Zack Davis on the *Firecracker*.
Photo by B. Garrity-Blake

Small
Fry

"Justin likes to have a mate," explained Zack Davis in the deliberate brogue of Down East speech. "Not me. I like to shrimp alone. No one talking your ear off or smart-mouthing you. Only thing you have to listen to is your engine." Zack did have a regular companion, though—a golden retriever named Whitey. "You can think out here, make your own decisions," the sixteen-year-old fisherman added.

Davis talked with the confidence of a seasoned waterman, a quality in stark contrast to his babyface. Two years earlier, Reverend Carpenter pointed to him during the Blessing of the Fleet as an example of a fisherman not long for this world. But the boy was still going strong and was thinking about buying a larger trawler.

"I started fishing about the same time I started kindergarten," he explained. First he worked with his uncle Randy Davis or his grandfather Bernie Davis, but by the time he was twelve he shrimped alone on the inky night waters of Core Sound in a boat his father built. Zack came from a family of boatbuilders and fishermen—his great-grandfather Ray Davis was a well-known builder of wooden "for-hire" headboats, sportfishing boats, skiffs, and trawlers.

"Some of us build 'em, some of us work 'em," said Zack, summing up the Davis family tradition.

Zack's boat, the *Firecracker*, a fire-engine-red, twenty-foot open-body skiff, had sailed in the North Carolina Seafood Festival's Blessing of the Fleet procession every year since 1997. His skiff looked impossibly small next to the menhaden vessels and cargo ships at the port. During the festival the teenager tied his boat near net menders and decoy carvers and politely juggled all sorts of curious questions from festive passersby. With his handsome looks and youthful enthusiasm, Zack demonstrated to tourists that commercial fishing is anything *but* a thing of the past.

Zack lived in Marshallberg and moored his boat in the harbor within eyeshot of his house. He was tied up next to a boat belonging to his friend and fishing buddy Justin Pigott. Justin, fifteen, also made his living on the water, sometimes with the help of ten-year-old Clayton Hancock, jokingly called "Cletus" by the older boys.

"We gonna catch us some bugs tonight, Cletus?" Zack asked, preparing for a Sunday night shrimp tow.

Clayton, a cheerful, round-faced fifth grader, stood on the dock passing gear to Justin. "Not if it's like the last time we went out!" he answered. It was early May, and the shrimp were still scarce.

"Cleeetus," grinned Zack. Justin, a tall, long-haired boy who wasn't inclined to say much, barely cracked a smile, intent on preparing for the night's tow.

Zack and Justin, sometimes joined by sixteen-year-old Brooks Heyland, kept watch over each other while working. This ring of fisherboys felt as though they had the whole world to themselves on the nights they shrimped together.

"Tonight's a school night," explained Zack, pulling away from the dock and heading out past a half-sunk boat. "But if I caught a hundred pounds right now, I'd not go to school tomorrow!" He rounded the mouth of the harbor and headed toward Brown's Island. "One night it started raining and everyone went in. Not me. I kept right on after the rain stopped, and the shrimp showed. I worked till daybreak and caught 200 pounds. My best night so far is 550 pounds."

Zack and Justin did pretty well with their small rigs—they each used a small trawl net, pulled in by hand.

"I made mine myself," remarked Zack. "Roger Harris to Atlantic cut it and I sewed it together the way I wanted it. If someone catches more shrimp than you, they'll try to figure out what's wrong with your rig. They'll help you get it right."

The lights of small trawlers appeared like fireflies as the sun went down. Most Core Sound trawlers were thirty-two to thirty-eight feet long and were rigged with double nets and mechanical winches. Because the boys pulled their nets in by hand, they were not required to outfit their trawls with turtle excluder devices.

"Not yet, anyway!" exclaimed Zack. He waved at a passing trawler. "I've not caught but one turtle in the last four and a half years, though. And buddy that turtle was ticked off from getting tangled in my net! I put him overboard but I don't reckon he was pleased about any of it."

A boatyard and marine railway sits on the southern end of Marshallberg. Several sportfishing boats, yachts, and fishing trawlers were up on blocks for repair. Twelve years ago the yard belonged to one of the biggest boat repair establishments in North Carolina, M.W. Willis and Son, where huge oceangoing trawlers and long-liners bumped their way through the shallows of Core Sound to get hauled out for wood-working, welding, and painting. Since M.W. Willis and Son closed, the yard looks modern, quiet, and too tidy.

Zack pointed at a trawler tied up at the far end of the marine railway. "That's a brand new boat. I'm getting ready to build a thirty-eight-footer. You can go anywhere in a boat that size. Rig her with bigger nets, a power winch– 'course, those can be dangerous. The cable can get little spurs on it that snag your glove and pull your hand right in. That's happened to a lot of people."

The boats that passed Zack were heading out to the Straits, their rigs silhouetted against the fading light, decks lit by a single bulb. Zack knew the names of every fisherman out there on that clear spring evening. "I trust this crowd right smart much," he said. "I break down, they come right to me. They break down, I do the same. Sometimes you get hung up. You have to put her out of gear and haul back. Could be an old broken-off piling or something. Sometimes it snags your tickler chain before it gets your net–that's what you hope for." The tickler chain was a metal chain that bumped along the bottom at the mouth of the net, causing the shrimp to jump out of the mud into the net.

"We pretty much follow the same towing patterns, though," said Zack. "It mainly gets bad after a hurricane or bad storm when all kinds of mess is in the water. We clean it out! But that's why we don't have a big law-enforcement problem around here, people going behind the lines, shrimping where they're not supposed to–we stick to the same areas as a rule."

Zack added, "I almost got a ticket once. Dean Nelson was waiting right there on the shore for me once because I was using the wrong color buoys on my gill net. You're supposed to have two yellow buoys on either end, with your name on them. We were using two orange ones we just found in the grass! I didn't argue with him, I was in the wrong. I just thanked him for the warning."

Once Zack was positioned to his satisfaction in the channel, he adjusted his net on the stern, aligning the two wooden "doors" that would spread the net open in the water. He yanked ropes and tied them off, all the while spinning his body around to steer the boat past shoals and buoys and to adjust the throttle to proper speed.

The net hit the water with a bubbly sigh. Zack took the helm and settled in for a peaceful tow, a crescent moon hanging in the dusky horizon. He, like his seasoned elders, loved commercial fishing, but he did not share their pessimistic outlook.

"The old-timers say there's no future in commercial fishing," he said, glancing back at his net and then forward towards a sandbar. "They've lived long enough to see all the changes, so it looks bad to them. Since my time, it's been no different, really. I'm *used* to all the rules and regulations. I don't get discouraged about it like the older crowd."

Zack maneuvered the *Firecracker* past the shoal and around back toward the harbor. "I am going to college, though," he said emphatically. "I'm going to NC State where my brother is now. Probably major in agriculture. It's good to have a backup in case they *do* close it down."

Zack was an honor student at East Carteret High School. He estimated that six or seven other high school boys and one girl operated their own shrimp boats. "My marine occupations teacher said 'raise your hand if you shrimp.' Two or three raised their hands. He said fifteen years ago two or three *didn't* shrimp! That's how it's changed. Mr. Weeks is my favorite. He teaches us all about the rules of fishing, navigation, building boats, rebuilding engines, reading charts–I've especially learned a lot about reading charts."

Zack laughed when asked if he brings his favorite teachers shrimp instead of an apple. "All the teachers I like catch their *own* shrimp."

As the *Firecracker* made a pass by the mouth of the harbor, where the lights from Zack's house were just visible, the dog poised himself on the bow. "Jump or don't jump, Whitey, make up your mind! Sometimes he jumps overboard and swims home when it gets dark," Zack explained. Whitey made a couple of false starts and then sprang off the bow into the water. He turned toward the *Firecracker*, then thought better of it and swam for shore.

"Yep," Zack continued, keeping an eye on Whitey and an oncoming shoal, "some say there ain't no living in commercial fishing. But it's like any other job; you've got to work at it to make it work. Those who say it ain't a good way to make a living don't work at it." He tossed his hand up to Justin and Clayton, passing in the opposite direction. Justin barely nodded his head, and Clayton waved enthusiastically. "You get out of it what you put in. Maybe not tonight, maybe not this month, but eventually you get paid."

Darkness had fallen, and the boys kept track of each other by the tiny light on each boat. Zack's mother Karen Davis worried about her son, alone at the helm all night long, especially during rainy blows. "She tells me, 'Don't get killed!' She says that a lot."

But Karen was also proud of the responsibilities her child took on. While other teens partied their summers away, these fisherkids worked under the constellations, learning in the moonlight and making serious money.

"I don't have a girlfriend right now," Zack shrugged. "Between my boat and my truck I have enough worries!"

Zack didn't mind too much, however, when Friday night was made off-limits to shrimping, giving the boys the whole weekend off. But his reasons were not selfish.

"I didn't think it was the end of the world to close Friday night. Don't get me wrong–I'm against all the closures and mess they're laying on fishermen. And a lot of it is just mess. But in that case, I didn't see the harm of giving the bottom an extra night of rest. It can't hurt."

Zack stood, preparing to haul back. He pulled the net, arm over arm, tying this rope off, untying that one, hauling with all his weight. Up came the tail bag, swinging from the pulleys with a small dripping load of grass, shrimp, crabs, and fish. "Nothing much," declared the captain. With that, the engine cut off. "What the? Don't tell me I've run out of gas." He flipped the plastic tank, and shook his head.

He looked across the water to a small light. "Justin and Clayton are probably hauling back. Well," he decided, "maybe I've got enough to start her and get back to the harbor."

He turned the key, and the *Firecracker* exploded forward. Zack, thrown toward the stern of the boat, grabbed the throttle on his way past and pulled the boat out of gear. The vessel stalled once again.

"This is exactly what I mean," he huffed, exasperated. "You make your own decisions out here, and your own mistakes. When you make a wrong one–and I've made plenty–you never forget it. I guarantee I will remember not to start the boat in gear again." He picked up his radio and tried to call Justin.

"Hey Justin. Heeeeeeeey Justin. C'mon, Justin." There was no response.

"Out here," he reflected, "it's different from someone telling you what to do, or reminding you all the time. You learn on your own, and remember what you learned!"

Zack gave up on the C.B. and switched his light on and off, on and off. Within minutes the distant glow of Justin's boat turned and headed toward the *Firecracker*. Zack explained that if nobody was nearby to help, he would simply anchor and swim to shore. "I've had to do that a time." He described a harrowing day when he was the only person on the water, making a run at the onset of Hurricane Bertha. "I made one quick tow in seventy-five-knot winds. I don't know if it was stupidity or deter- mination, but I caught a hundred pounds of shrimp!"

"I've been in plenty of storms," he continued. "You can get struck by lightning in the parking lot of Wal-Mart as easy as here. I just figure," the teenager sighed, looking up at the moon, "if it's my time to go, it's my time to go." He glanced over at Justin and Clayton, who were fast approaching. "But you ain't really out here alone."

"What happened?" asked Clayton, standing on the bow of Justin's boat.

"Ran out of gas," said Zack, with an embarrassed smile.

"You're purty!" grinned Justin, his voice cracking.

"First words I heard out of you all night," Zack shot back.

Justin towed the *Firecracker* to a bank at the mouth of Marshallberg Harbor, where he slid the bow of both vessels up on the grass. Since Justin had already culled his catch, he donned a full slicker and hood. He shook out his net, swabbed his deck, and rubbed off every little smudge until his boat was gleaming and spotless.

Clayton helped Zack cull the *Firecracker's* catch, which lay glistening and moving on the culling table. "Watch out for the knucklebusters," warned Zack, referring to a shrimp-like creature that resembled an army tank. "They don't call 'em that for nothing. Be glad we didn't catch a starlight fish. Touch him between the eyes and it's just like sticking your finger in a light socket!" They tossed the fish, crabs, knucklebusters, and squid overboard and popped the heads off the shrimp.

"If we catch a big load, mamma heads 'em and sells 'em while I'm in school," Zack explained. "I've got the fishing license, she's got the dealer license." He poured his shrimp in with Justin's. "Me and Justin combine and split fifty-fifty on nights like this."

It was about nine o'clock when the shrimp was culled. While most kids were doing last-minute homework or watching Sunday night television, these boys were assessing their luck and finishing business. "Run out of gas! Da*ggone* it!" Zack remarked while shaking out his net. "Sounds like something Cletus would do."

"But you're the one who *did* do it, Zack," observed the ten-year-old matter-of-factly.

"Cleeeetus," said Zack, grinning.

After he finished swabbing his deck with buckets of salt water, Zack held two shrimp in his hand. "See this with the spot on him? He's what you call a spotted shrimp. We don't catch much of them to speak of, but they're the first to show in the spring. See this one without the spot? That there's a summer shrimp. See here, Cletus? Summer shrimp are starting to show! Those are the ones we're waiting for. Then come the greentails."

"When are they gonna show, Zack?" asked Clayton.

"Here's my big theory," said Zack. "On a flood tide, they go to the bottom. On an ebb, they come to the top. And on a full moon, they get out of the mud and go to the creeks, the sounds, and out to the ocean headed to South Carolina. Shrimp *run* on a full moon. And that's when we put her in the meat and go." Clayton listened intently.

"Ain't that right, Cletus? Put her in the meat and go! Cletus! Look at the moon. Tell me how many days till she's full."

Clayton regarded the crescent. "Ah, five days?"

"Five days?!" exclaimed Zack. "Cleeeeetus. It'll take a little longer than that. But when she's full, we'll catch us some bugs then, won't we buddy?"

Zack, Brooks, and Justin sorting their catch.
Photo by B. Garrity-Blake

Jail boom truck.
Photo by B. Garrity-Blake

Epilogue

"Clammer Bob" Worthington continues to strive for a simple life, so was compelled to trade his clam rake for a hammer. His concerns about the far-reaching effects of governmental control are shared more than ever throughout the fishing industry. The North Carolina Fisheries Reform Act was not the "search and destroy" mechanism some feared and has brought about the involvement of more watermen, sportsmen, and other citizens in the management of marine resources than in other states. But the stepped-up involvement of regional and federal agencies such as the Atlantic States Marine Fisheries Commission and the National Marine Fisheries Service makes the state's new and improved management system less relevant, as the Tarheel state must comply with overarching plans not always in the state's interest.

Although Willie Etheridge's heart grows cold at the mere mention of the federal agency, he believes there are a few folks there, not to mention a politician or two, who will listen to the few remaining "pirates" of the world—he keeps the trail warm from Wanchese to Washington, D.C.

Lonnie Trinh continues to strut her stuff, controlling three boats and a whopping 2,400 crab pots despite poor forecasts for fishermen. She still sells her catch to Willy Phillips, who admits he has moments when he misses serving on the state's fisheries board. The crabbing industry has changed dramatically in the past couple of years—not because of the state's new management plan, but because of natural and global factors. The record harvests of the late 1990s tumbled after a series of hurricanes wreaked havoc on the natural environment, especially the floodwaters of Floyd, which breached hog lagoons and wastewater plants, dumping hundreds of millions of gallons of pollutants into the rivers and sounds. By 2000, a man-made disaster hit the industry. Half of the picking houses in North Carolina shut their doors after imported Asian crabmeat infiltrated the market and gobbled up 80 percent of the market share. Some processors, such as fisheries commissioner Jimmy Johnson, were compelled to tack into the shifting winds of a global market and now promote "value-added" blended products made up of wild, farm-grown, domestic, and even imported seafood. "Crab Jalapeno Popums" and "Buffalo Catfish Nuggets," packaged for consumer convenience and a longer shelf life, seem to be the wave of the future.

Shrimpers like Milton Styron have adjusted to Turtle Excluder Devices, or switched to "skimmer rigs," which do not require TEDs. Other fisheries are feeling sea turtle-protection pressures–the threat of a lawsuit from an environmental organization inspired the National Marine Fisheries Service to ban flounder gill nets in the deep waters of Pamlico Sound, displacing some fishermen and rendering null and void a state-sponsored study of gill-net-turtle interactions. The federal agency also ignored a system designed by monkfish fishermen to avoid the unintentional capture of migrating sea turtles and instead closed the fishery down in Tarheel waters. "Standing up to these kinds of politics is a matter of life and death to me," said Styron, now in his eighties and still working.

Since the *News and Observer* no longer runs Joel Arrington's inflammatory sports columns, fishermen are less inclined to use the paper as a mullet wrapper. But mullets are now wrapped in the slicker paper of several large sport-fishing magazines, which carry Arrington and other columnists touting the banning of nets and the designation of red drum as "gamefish only." State officials estimate that the number of sport fishermen frequenting North Carolina waters has doubled to two million in the last decade. Although the majority of anglers do not subscribe to the anticommercial rhetoric of some lobby groups, their sheer impact on marine resources is a growing concern for state officials. Commercial fishermen are wary of a proposed recreational fishing license, watching other states like Texas, which just added a three-dollar surcharge to its sportfishing stamp for the express purpose of buying back and retiring commercial licenses to "reduce stress" on the environment.

Leon Scarborough still sets nets in Pamlico Sound but can also be found fishing for fun on the beach near Hatteras Inlet. Several of the recreational fishermen who post messages on the FishMoJo website drop by to visit him when they're on the island. With tighter federal control looming on the horizon, Leon and other Outer Banks fishermen don't believe they'll ever see the return of a viable commercial fishery for red drum.

Even though gray trout is now classified as healthy and is no longer listed as over-fished, the balmy winter of 2002 saw few fish off Hatteras Island. The low volume of trout, coupled with a federal management plan that amounted to a shut-down of dogfish harvesting in the state, were factors leading Quality Seafood to stop sending their truck to Michael Peele's fish house after twenty-six years. Fishermen held their breath, waiting to see if Peele would sell out to a real-estate tycoon eyeing the waterfront property, but Peele stuck to his promise and leased the building to another fish dealer in the village. Only a few North Carolina fishermen heard a biologist tell the Atlantic State Marine Fisheries Commission, the group that had called for a 75-percent reduction in gray trout harvest, that recruitment had gone up steadily over the last decade and that the fishery had been in good shape after all, even before substantial regulations were imposed.

Frustration with fisheries data has pushed more fishermen into cooperative research partnerships with scientists. Andy Read, the Duke University scientist whose initial interaction with North Carolina fishermen was marred by a lack of communication, has become a leader in those new partnerships. Fishermen worked with Read on an aerial survey of dolphin in North Carolina's estuaries. The survey results cast a shadow on NMFS's estimate of the number of bottlenose. Read and fishermen are examining the interaction of dolphins with fishing nets, and they will test alterations in net design, including the addition of pingers. Unlike the Harbor Porpoise Take Reduction Team described in chapter 9, the Bottlenose Dolphin Take Reduction Team plan reached full consensus. But NMFS has balked at implementing the team's recommendations, resisting their own data showing a much larger population of bottlenose than previous estimates.

Patrick Hill and other Core Sounders will likely see more shellfish leases off their shores, as legislators are expected to lift the moratorium and allow controlled expansion of the program. Aquaculture is severely impacting "wild" fishermen in terms of the global market. Asian and Central American shrimp farms targeted the U.S. market in 2002, after European nations banned pond-raised shrimp due to high levels of antibiotics found in the product. Although Tarheel fishermen are harvesting a bumper crop, they find prices paltry due to 90 percent of the market share going to cheap imported shrimp. Fishermen from several Gulf and Atlantic states are filing an antidumping lawsuit against countries that are able to undercut prices with low labor costs and weak environmental regulations.

The menhaden factory at the end of Taylor's Creek in Beaufort is still clanking away, "held together by rust," shore engineer Elwood Willis says. Levi Beveridge has been dead fifteen years, but small piles of cat food are everywhere in daily memorial to the old net mender. Jule Wheatly and other Atlantic coast menhaden representatives lost their membership on the Atlantic Menhaden Management Board, as Atlantic States Marine Fisheries Commission members voted to kick industry off the panel despite years of success in working with scientists and policy-makers. They now have reduced input into the regulations affecting their operations at a time when more states push to have the "unsightly" vessels prohibited off their shores. Wheatly continues to predict that this is the company's last season, and his captains and their crew keep proving him wrong.

The Chowan River pound-netters survived another slow herring season. At least one management insider quietly whispers that he doesn't believe the restrictions on fishermen will bring the herring back, pointing out that the physical landscape has been altered so much that acres of spawning ground have vanished.

Zack Davis began his first year of college and missed out on the fall shrimp run, but figured he "got the best of summer" anyway. His buddy Justin has become a full-time commercial fisherman, and captains a trawler off Snead's Ferry and other points east. Zack made it home to run his new vessel in the Seafood Festival's Blessing of the Fleet. The *Firecracker II* promises to earn him enough money this summer to carry him through the next semester and beyond.

Thanks to the hard work of women like Sandra Gaskill, this year's Blessing of the Fleet tightened the line fishing families have to the larger coastal community. Sandra proudly noted that more young fishermen took part in the ceremony. Everyone agreed that Pastor Carpenter would have enjoyed the day. Carpenter answered God's call and now ministers in a small mill town near Rockingham in the Piedmont Plateau, but holds Cedar Island close to his heart and harbors no regrets over his days as a fisheries activist. "I suppose my activism took me, more than anyone, by surprise, but I saw that the truth needed to be told," said Carpenter. "One thing I can say for sure is that I raised some heck."

Sources

Boom Truck Heaven

Butler, Ed. "Boom Truck Has its Day." *Carteret County News-Times*, 12 February 1999.

Carpenter, Robert L. Jr. "Letter to the Editor." *Carteret County News-Times*, 28 February 1999.

____. "Letter to the Editor." *Carteret County News-Times*, 14 October 1998.

Kemp, Rodney, and Sonny Williamson. Program on FM 107 WTKF, October 1998.

Saunders, Doc. "Letter to the Editor." *Carteret County News-Times*, 22 February 1998.

Simpson, Thelma. Interview by Barbara Garrity-Blake, 11 March 1986.

A Simple Clammer

North Carolina Fisheries Moratorium Steering Committee. Letters received, 1995-1997.

Richardson, Representative Billy. Letter to Robert Lucas, Chairman, North Carolina Marine Fisheries Commission, 23 March 1995.

Richissin, Todd. "Panel Votes Down Overhaul of Fishing Rules." *The News and Observer*, 11 February 1997.

Worthington, "Clammer Bob." Interview by Barbara Garrity-Blake, 16 March 1999.

La Casa de Jaiba

"Commission Listens, But Unable to Help Crabbers with Perceived Problems." *The Coastland Times*, 24 May 1994.

Garrity-Blake, Barbara. Interviews at Full Circle Crab Co., Alligator, North Carolina, 10 September 2001.

Griffith, David. *The Estuary's Gift: An Atlantic Coast Cultural Biography*. University Park: Pennsylvania State University Press, 1999.

Hinson, Glenn. *Virginia Worksongs*. Blue Ridge Institute Records 007, 1983.

Stancil, Nancy. "N.C. Crabbers Seek Protection." *The Charlotte Observer*, 22 April 1994.

This Pirate

Basnight, Marc. "Letter to the Editor." *The News and Observer*, 17 November 1997.

DeGregory, Lane. "Watermen and Anglers at Odds Over Billfish." *The Virginian-Pilot*, 5 October 1997.

Glass, Jon. "Called Illegal, $40,000 Tuna is Trashed." *The Virginian-Pilot*, 25 June 1992.

Griffin, Anna. "Basnight is the Power the State Seldom Sees." *The Charlotte Observer*, 27 January 2001.

North Carolina Division of Marine Fisheries. Public Meeting Transcripts, 3 May 2000.

Oden, Jeff. "Letter to the Editor." *Carteret County News-Times*, 29 May 1998.

Paul, Bruce. "Sea Striker Reels in Nearly $1 Million." *Carteret County News-Times*, 17 June 2001.

Rich, Brad. "Scientist Disputes Big Rock Claims." *Carteret County News-Times*, 24 October 1997.

Semans, Sandy. "Something Fishy." *The Pamlico News*, 15 October 1997.

"Tuna Dispute Puts Dead Fish on the Road." *Coastland Times*, 25 June 1992.

Red Herring

Associated Press. "Full Review Sought for Hertford Steel Mill." *The News and Observer*, 17 July 1999.

Baity, Crystal. Letter to Preston Pate, Director of the North Carolina Marine Fisheries Commission, 10 March 2000.

Basnight, Marc. Speech on the North Carolina Senate Floor during Debate on the Fisheries Reform Act, 11 August 1997.

Brame, Richen. Letter to Robert V. Lucas, Chairman, North Carolina Marine Fisheries Commission, 20 March 1996.

Byrum, Herbert Ray, Terry Pratt, Lennie Perry, and C.S. Tynch Jr. Letter to Bruce Freeman, 16 February 1996.

Clayborne, Jonathan. "Jamesville Looks for Help in Saving Herring Festival." *Washington Daily News*, 3 March 2000.

DeGregory, Lane. "Herring Fest Will Go On Without Fresh Fish." *The Virginian-Pilot*. 2 March 1995.

____. "Empty Nets." *The Coast*, 5 March 1995.

____. "Despite Compromise, Fishermen Are Still Fighting Herring Limits." *The Virginian-Pilot*. 10 April 1996.

Evans-Stanton, Sherri. Letter to Jimmy Johnson, Chairman, North Carolina Marine Fisheries Commission, 16 August 1999.

Freeman, Bruce. Letter to Albemarle Sound Fishermen, 4 April 1996.

Gray, Betty Mitchell. "Commission Severely Restricts Season for Herring and Shad." *The Virginian-Pilot*, 4 December 1994.

____. "Local Herring and Shad Fishermen Face Restricted Seasons." *The Virginian-Pilot*, 25 August 1994.

Hackney, C., J. Grimley, M. Posey, and T. Alphin. "Sediment Contamination in North Carolina's Estuaries." Wilmington: University of North Carolina at Wilmington, 2 October 1998.

Johnson, H.B. and et al. "Biology and Management of Mid-Atlantic Anadromous Fishers Under Extended Jurisdiction." North Carolina Department of Natural Resources and Community Development, Division of Marine Fisheries, Morehead City, 1981.

McDonald, Marshall. "The Rivers and Sounds of North Carolina." In *The Fisheries and Fishery Industries of the United States*, vol. 1, edited by George Brown Goode. Washington, D.C.: Government Printing Office, 1887.

North Carolina Marine Fisheries Commission. Transcript of Business Meeting, 17 March 1995.

_____. Transcript of Business Meeting, 3 December 1994.

Simpson, Bland, and Ann Cary Simpson. *Into the Sound Country: A Carolinian's Coastal Plain*. Chapel Hill: University of North Carolina Press, 1997.

Street, Michael W., and Jackson Davis. "Assessment of United States Atlantic Coast River Herring Fishery." Paper presented to the International Commission for the Northwest Atlantic Fisheries, 5 March 1976.

Street, Michael W., and Harrel B. Johnson. "Status of the Commercial Fisheries of the Albemarle Sound Area." North Carolina Department of Natural Resources and Community Development, Division of Marine Fisheries, Morehead City, August 1982.

Warner, William W. *Distant Water: The Fate of the North Atlantic Fisherman*. Boston: Little, Brown and Co., 1977.

Yocum, Thomas. "Fishing Group Hits Herring Decision." *Outer Banks Sentinel*, 4 April 1996.

Turtle Stew

Beacham, Tina. "Letter to the Editor." *Carteret County News-Times*, 13 October 1992.

Garrity-Blake, Barbara. "To Fish or Not to Fish: Occupational Transitions within the Commercial Fishing Community of Carteret County, NC." Raleigh: North Carolina Sea Grant, 1996.

Gillikin, Linda. "Letter to the Editor." *Carteret County News-Times*, 15 February 2002.

Island Born and Bred. Harkers Island: United Methodist Women, 1987.

Knudson, Tom. "Litigation Central: A Flood of Costly Lawsuits Raises Questions About Motive." *The Sacramento Bee*, 24 April 2001.

National Academy of the Sciences. *Decline of the Sea Turtles: Causes and Prevention*. Washington, D.C.: National Academy Press, 1990.

Rich, Brad. "Fishermen's Wives, Girls Form Auxiliary: Fight for Their Men." *Carteret County News-Times*, 7 June 1992.

Sharpe, Benjamin S. Letter to Beverly Perdue, *North Carolina Senator*, April 1994.

True, Frederick W. "The Turtle and Terrapin Fisheries." In *The Fisheries and Fishery Industries of the United States*, sect. 2, part 11, edited by George Brown Goode. Washington, D.C.: Government Printing Office, 1887.

The Mullet Wrapper

Arrington, Joel. "Netters in North Carolina Are Allowed to Snatch Public Resources From Anglers." *The News and Observer*, 20 December 1992.

DeGregory, Lane. "Feud Over a Declining Resource." *The Coast*, 8 November 1992.

——. "Fishermen Meet to Settle Old Feuds." *The Virginian-Pilot*, 7 January 1993.

——. "Commercial Fishermen Lose a New Surf War." *The Virginian-Pilot*, 18 August 1993.

Hogarth, William T. Letter to Steve C. Sink, 29 March 1993.

Hutchinson, Bob. "There Is No Longer Enough to Go Around." *The Virginian-Pilot*, 14 January. 1993.

Kellum, Sandra. "Letter to the Editor." *Carteret County News-Times*, 30 January 1993.

"Letters to the Editor." *The News and Observer*, 10 January 1993.

Mid-Atlantic Fishery Management Council. "Fishery Management Plan for the Bluefish Fishery." May 1989.

Muse, Suellen. "Letter to the Editor." *The News and Observer*, 10 January 1993.

National Park Service. "Commercial/Recreational Fishing Discussion Paper." August 1993.

Schill, Jerry. Letter to Mayor Renee Cahoon of Nag's Head, 1 February 1993.

Sink, Steve. Letter to Bill Hogarth, 14 March 1993.

Stick, David. *The Outer Banks of North Carolina*. Chapel Hill: University of North Carolina Press, 1958.

West, Susan. "Bob Swartz: Fishing Has Been His Life." *The Island Breeze*, June 1997.

Williams, Ted. "Murder in the Nursery: North Carolina Needs to Grow Up and Let Juvenile Fish do the Same." *Fly Rod and Reel* (November/December 1997): 17-22.

Fish House Opera

Atlantic States Marine Fisheries Commission. Transcript of Joint Weakfish Management Board and Advisory Panel Meeting. Alexandria, Virginia, 16 March 1999.

Oden, Jeff. "New Regulations for Weakfish Based On Faulty Assumptions." *The Island Breeze*, April 1994.

West, Susan. "A Disturbing Saga of How Federal Bureaucrats Ignore the Truth." *The Island Breeze*, April 1996.

____. "Hatteras Fish Houses Are the Heart of the Local Industry." *The Island Breeze*, September 2000.

Fish Doctors

Allegood, Jerry. "Dolphin Makes Miraculous Recovery." *The News and Observer*, 12 October 1995.

Anderson, Eric, et al. Letter to Rolland Schmitten, National Marine Fisheries Service, 2 September 1997.

Corey, Tony. "Untangling the Issue to Save the Whales." *Nor'easter, Magazine of the Northeast Sea Grant Programs* (1998).

Gray, Landry, and Ralph Umphlett. "Porpoising along the Outer Banks in the early 1900s." *The Sea Chest* 4, no. 3 (Spring 1978): 38-41.

Gulf of Maine/Bay of Fundy Harbor Porpoise Take Reduction Team. "Final Draft Report of Gulf of Maine/Bay of Fundy Harbor Porpoise

Take Reduction Plan." 7 August 1996.

Kraus, S., and A. Read. "A Field Test of the Use of Acoustic Alarms to Reduce Mortality of Harbor Porpoises in Gill Nets." Draft Final Report, 20 April 1995.

Prioli, Carmine, and Edwin Martin. *Hope for a Good Season*. Asheboro: Down Home Press, 1998.

Read, Dr. Andrew. Letter to Rolland Schmitten, National Marine Fisheries Service, 9 September 1997.

Salsi, Lynn, and Frances Eubanks. *Carteret County*. Charleston: Arcadia Publishing, 1999.

Sargent, Anne. "Whale Is Rescued off Cape Lookout." *Carteret County News-Times*, 6 April 1995.

South, Paul. "Rescuers Free Whale from Net off Pea Island." *Virginian Pilot*, 5 December 1994.

Young, Sharon B. Letter to Rolland Schmitten, National Marine Fisheries Service, 8 September 1997.

A Penny Hurts

Brooks, Dale. Interview by Barbara Garrity-Blake, 26 August 1995.

Krantz, Les. *Jobs Rated Almanac*. Ft. Lee, N.J.: Barricade Books, 2002.

Rich, Brad. "Wives also See and Feel Sea Change in Fishing." *Carteret County News-Times*, 16 June 1995.

Tosto, Mike and Edwina. Interview by Barbara Garrity-Blake, 15 June 1995.

Wave of the Future

Cobey, William Jr. Letter to Susan Salter, 6 August 1992.

Green, Ann. "The Vanishing Oyster." *Coastwatch*, North Carolina Sea Grant, Winter 2000.

Hogarth, William. Letter to W. Willis, 1 July 1992.

North Carolina Blue Ribbon Advisory Council on Oysters. Minutes, 7 November 1994.

North Carolina Blue Ribbon Advisory Council on Oysters. "Final Report on Studies and Recommendations," 1 October 1995.

North Carolina Division of Marine Fisheries. Public Hearing Transcripts, 8 April 1996.

North Carolina Division of Marine Fisheries. Letters Protesting Proposed Lease #9201.

North Carolina Division of Marine Fisheries. Letters Protesting Proposed Leases #9515, 9516, 9517, 9519, 9521, 9525, 9526.

North Carolina Division of Marine Fisheries. Memorandum to Director on Supplementary Investigation of Proposed Shellfish Leases 9515, 9516, 9517, and 9519 in Core Sound, 8 April 1996.

North Carolina Division of Marine Fisheries. Proceedings from the Public Forum on Cleaning Up Coastal Waters for Oystering and Clamming, 14 March 2000.

Rich, Brad. "Clammers Harvest Future Crop." *Carteret County News-Times*, 20 June 1993.

Salter, Susan. Letter to William Cobey, Jr., 8 July 1992.

Red Drum

Arrington, Joel. "More Protection Needed for Red Drum." *The News and Observer*, 26 October 1997.

_____. "Marching to the Beat of Red Drum." *The News and Observer*, 25 July 1994.

Daniel, Louis, Lee Paramore, and John Carmichael. "Marine Fisheries Commission Information Paper–Red Drum Assessment." North Carolina Division of Marine Fisheries, 28 July 1998.

Fulcher, Murray. "Letter to the Editor." *Carteret County News-Times*, 9 October 1998.

Hutchinson, Bob. "Fishing Forecast." *The Virginian-Pilot*, 15 October 1998.

North Carolina Marine Fisheries Commission. Public Meeting and Business Session, New Bern, 9 September 1998.

Moffitt, Pete. "Letter to the Editor." *Carteret County News-Times*, 16 September 1998.

West, Susan. "Fisheries Managers Learn from the Fishermen." *The Island Breeze*, June 1999.

_____. "A Conversation with a Hatteras Fisherman." *The Island Breeze*, June 2001.

Pogie Boat

Garrity-Blake, Barbara. Fieldnotes. January, 1986.

_____. *The Fish Factory*. Knoxville: University of Tennessee Press, 1994.

Blessings

Carpenter, Robert L. Jr. "Letter to the Editor." *Carteret County News-Times*, 28 February 1999.

Garrity-Blake, Barbara. Interviews aboard the *William H. Smith*, 3 October 1999.

Kemp, Rodney, and Sonny Williamson. Program on FM 107 WTKF, October 1998.

Night Trawl

Jenson, Chris. "Comments Pertaining to Observer Work on a Shrimp Trawler Working in Core Sound, North Carolina during June/July 1993." Report delivered to National Marine Fisheries Service, 1993.

Styron, Milton. Conversations with Barbara Garrity-Blake, 1995-2002.

_____. "Ode to the Fisherman." North Carolina Seafood Festival Blessing of the Fleet Program, 1999.

Small Fry

Davis, Zack, and Friends. Interviews by Barbara Garrity-Blake, Marshallberg Harbor, April 2000, August 2000, September 2002.

About the
Authors

Barbara Garrity-Blake is author of *The Fish Factory* (University of Tennessee Press, 1994), an ethnohistorical study of the menhaden fishery of North Carolina and Virginia. She is the author of several academic articles, and has written op-ed columns in *The News and Observer*. She holds a Ph.D. in anthropology, and taught for nine years at East Carolina University. She lives in coastal Carolina with her husband, a boatbuilder and musician. Garrity-Blake has worked with the grassroots movement of fishermen, serving with the Carteret Auxiliary of the North Carolina Fisheries Association and TWINE (Tarheel Watermen for Industry, Nature, and Education). She served on the state Fisheries Moratorium Steering Committee, and now she shapes policy as a member of the North Carolina Marine Fisheries Commission.

Susan West is the wife of a Hatteras Island commercial fisherman. She writes the "Fishing for a Living" column in *The Island Breeze*. She is well respected for her work in fisheries management, including her service on the North Carolina Fisheries Moratorium Steering Committee. West has served as president of the Hatteras-Ocracoke Auxiliary of the North Carolina Fisheries Association, a grassroots women-led activist group advocating citizen participation in management. She has brought fishing issues to the public's attention, speaking at the North Carolina Seafood Festival, the North Carolina Recreational Fishing Forum, and a U.S. Senate subcommittee hearing.

ALSO PUBLISHED BY MYSTIC SEAPORT

Voyages: Stories of America and the Sea
Andrew W. German

This companion to the exhibit *Voyages: Stories of America and the Sea* offers short overview essays, timelines, and illustrations drawn from the exhibit. Designed for family enjoyment and student reference, it includes a select reading list and a directory of American maritime museums. The book's seven chapters follow the exhibit's thematic structure, reflecting the principal ways the sea touches our lives. Mystic Seaport proudly presents *Voyages: Stories of America and the Sea*, an exhibit designed to reveal how the sea touches you, your family, and our nation.

(1999) 8 1/4" x 11 3/4", 96 pages, illustrations, photographs.
ISBN 0-913372-91-9 (paper)

BHZ006
$15.95

America and the Sea - *A Maritime History*
William M. Fowler, Jr.
Andrew W. German
John B. Hattendorf
Benjamin W. Labaree
Jeffrey J. Safford
Edward W. Sloan

America and the Sea: A Maritime History is the most comprehensive maritime history of the United States available today. Spanning the centuries from Native American and Viking maritime activities before Columbus through today's maritime enterprise, the text provides a new history of the U.S. from the fundamental perspective of the sea that surrounds it and the rivers and lakes that link its vast interior to the seacoast. *America and the Sea* has been gracefully written by six prominent maritime-history scholars whose individual areas of research and teaching range from labor to technology, from the fisheries to the U.S. Navy. Their text incorporates considerations of art, literature and poetry along with discussions of the economic, political, diplomatic and technological foundations of American maritime history. Their narrative is punctuated and augumented with quotations from period documents, and with brief essays by younger scholars that add insight and expand on the human dimensions of America's relationship with the sea. This rich, complex story is told not only in words but with 71 color images, many of them paintings from museums around the world, with 289 archival photographs and drawings in black and white, and with 10 full color maps.

(1998) 9" x 12", x plus 694 pages, 360 photographs
and drawings, maps, appendix, bibliography, index.
ISBN 0-913372-81-1 (cloth)

PUB811X
$65.00

Booksellers and libraries should order this book from: Independent Publishers Group, Order Department, 814 North Franklin Street, Chicago, IL 60610; telephone (800) 888-4741 and fax (312) 337-5985. Retail orders may be made to Mystic Seaport's bookstore - (800) 331-2665.

"A model of popular scholarship, and clearly the definitive work on the subject."

– Kirkus Reviews

"Abundantly illustrated with photos, graphs, and full-color maps, this is essential for all libraries."

– Library Journal

Fish House Opera

Susan West *and*
Barbara J. Garrity-Blake

Fishing families live by the values considered truly American: independence, risk-taking, and honest hard work. Yet, in the competition over uses of the sea and protection of its resources, fishermen often become victims rather than equal participants in the search for solutions.

Taking place in 16 "acts" on and beside the broad waters of North Carolina, *Fish House Opera* offers eloquent testimony on the issues facing commercial fishing families today.

Here they share their delight in being fully engaged in a life well-lived and their despair at seeing that way of life changed beyond their control. With all of the comic and tragic elements of a classic opera, *Fish House Opera* will resonate with anyone seeking to comprehend the nature of American life at the beginning of the twenty-first century.